Aurea Vidyā Collection*

———— 2 ————

*For a complete list of Titles, see page 179.

AT THE SOURCE OF LIFE

This book was originally published in Italian
as: Raphael, *Alle Fonti della Vita*, Domande e risposte sull'ultima Realtà, by
Associazione Ecoculturale Parmenides (formerly Edizioni Āśram Vidyā),
Rome.
Sixth Edition 2011

First published in English in 2001 by Aurea Vidyā
39 West 88th Street, New York, N.Y. 10024, U.S.A.
www.vidya-ashramvidyaorder.org

© Āśram Vidyā 1979

Printed and bound by Lighntning Source Inc. at locations in the U.S.A and in the U.K., as shown on the last page.

No part of this book may be reproduced in any form without the written permission from the publisher except for the quotation of brief passages in criticism, citing the source.

The revenues from the sale of this books, for which there are no copyright obligations, will be used for re-prints.

ISBN 979-8-576124-75-6
Library of Congress Control Number: 2002100516

On the cover: Orphic Gold-leaf Tablet, V-IV Century b.c., found in
 Hipponion (Vibo Valentia, Italy).
 Museo Archeologico di Vibo Valentia, Italy.

RAPHAEL
(Āśram Vidyā Order)

AT THE SOURCE OF LIFE

Questions and Answers
concerning the Ultimate Reality

Aurea Vidyā

Tell them,
'I am daughter of Earth and starry Sky,
and of heaven is my race; and of this you too
are well aware. I burn and waste away
with thirst; but give me straightway
of that cool water which flows from
the lake of Mnemosyne.'
They will let you drink at the divine spring.

Orphic Tablet of Petelia

TABLE OF CONTENTS

Introduction	13
AT THE SOURCE OF LIFE	23
Man's Ideal	25
True Love	29
Man's Enemy	31
The Limits of the Mind	35
We are the Children of Desire	45
Reality, the Absolute	54
Evolutionism	65
The Teacher	69
The Awakened Man	73
Advaita	77
Subject and Object	82
Time	91
Immortality and Bliss	95
There are various Pathways	99
Occultism and Psychical Powers	101
Art	107
THE PATHWAY OF FIRE	109
Contemplation of Action	111
Jīvanmukta	119

Contd.

Brahman	127
Freedom and Slavery	139
Education	145
Projection	149
Solution	153
Path of Awakening	159
Translation of the Gold-leaf Tablet shown on the Cover	165
Raphael: Unity of Tradition	169

INTRODUCTION

Every work of Raphael is precious because it represents an important means, a relevant channel which gives many people the opportunity of hearing a voice that, especially here in the West, may prove of invaluable help especially to those in search of a practical way of realization.

The first part of *At the Source of Life* is presented in dialogue form. Wherever there is a question there is a void that needs to be filled, a lack of knowledge to be met, a doubt to be clarified, and hence a truth that needs only to be revealed, because since 'all is within ourselves', that truth, too, will be found in the depths of our being. With this certainty as his starting-point, Raphael often answers one question with another question, and with a skill akin to Socrates' maieutic art, obliges the questioner to retreat further and further into himself, until the answer he was seeking is brought forth into the light.

Let us now look at the subject-matter of the text, which depicts the whole of man's psychical and intellectual make-up, indicates his ideals, his deviations, and his weaknesses, traces his conflicts and sufferings to their causes, and at the same time investigates Ultimate Reality as well as man's position with regard to it.

The deep analysis opens up unexpected horizons: the discussion branches out in unforeseen directions and touches on unexplored summits. What is set forth right at the beginning is the concept of comprehension. Comprehension is love, that love which since Christ's death has never again blossomed 'in the hearts of men'.

Love here is meant not in the egotistical *do ut des* sense (to give in order to receive), but in the sense of total giving without ever asking, that is 'Joy without desire'. Yes, true Love must give, but what can one give if one's hands are empty, if one's heart is arid and one's mind is filled with egoism. Therefore, let us first seek to enrich ourselves and 'fill our knapsacks' by rediscovering the true values of life; let us transform ourselves and realize those values. Only when we ourselves own this wealth shall we be able to be true givers.

In order to transform ourselves we must know and study ourselves, understand who our enemies are and fight them. Very often we are unable to recognize them and, sometimes, when we evaluate our mistakes, we tend to attribute to an object the importance that we should rather give to our reaction to it. This consideration is of great relevance and may have incalculable consequences both for society and for each one of us as to how we live our own lives.

Very often we blame most of our anxieties, our anguish, and above all our stress, on the technical bent of present-day society. If instead of blaming progress we were to examine our own reaction to the products of progress we would see that we are free to accept them either with indifference or with attachment. In the first case, detaching ourselves from the consumer mentality which drags us into a vortex of needs and forces us to adopt a mad pace of life that causes so much alienation and neurosis, we would remain calm and at peace, in the second, we would feel obliged to engage in a dizzy race to possess them! Let us, therefore, allow for science and man's intelligence to develop along their own paths, and let us rather balance our own reactions. In this manner we shall assume an appropriate standpoint of consciousness towards desire, we who are 'children of desire'.

In fact, desires of all kinds and of all magnitudes limit us and direct our energies, nailing us down to conflict, suffering, and incompleteness.

All philosophies have dealt with the problem of desire. Raphael offers a solution to the problem by identifying clearly, and above all with the aim of realization, the following steps: embracing the desire, mastering it, directing it, and transcending it: 'one who has transcended desire in all its forms is with the gods.'

So far we have followed the transformation of man through the action of comprehension, love and the release of desire. Now we have to understand why this transformation is necessary. It is because we wish to acknowledge our true nature, our deepest reality, which is absolute Consciousness and Bliss beyond the world of becoming and change.

But this sublime yearning will not be realized unless we proceed with the total transformation of ourselves, with discrimination between the real and the unreal, unless we aim at Truth with all our strength, devoting ourselves completely to the task of revelation rather than to that of evolution, to discover within ourselves what we have always been: the *ātman*, which, according to the teaching of the *Upaniṣads* or *Vedānta*, as expounded by Raphael with outstanding clarity, is the absolute within us.

Each theme dealt with causes others to emerge, and our search extends into ever-increasing circles. We have mentioned becoming, i.e. the fleeting world of change. This leads us to reflect upon the fact that this is where man, or rather the ego-body-mind complex normally seeks the solution to his problems and hopes for happiness. In this book no specific chapter has been devoted to it, but this ego with all its deceit, its alibis, and its treachery, is always present, which is why Raphael underlines its incompleteness, its dishonesty, its falseness, and its cunning, with a feeling close to pity for trapped consciousness of anyone who is a victim of the ego and is unable to escape from it. If we wish to proceed along the pathway of liberation and uncover our nature as that of the *ātman*, solving the problem of the ego is an indispensable step.

There is no other way of neutralizing the potency of the ego because even by giving it further power we could never rectify its constitutional weakness and poverty: rather would it use its new strength to make us even more slavish.

Throughout the book there is continuous mention of the mind; one whole chapter is dedicated to the complexity of the mental processes, and the mind is seen as a limited tool for perceiving external data. Being unable to turn to face the knowing subject ('Nobody can dance on his own shoulders'), the mind begins its work of projection and creates the ego, time, space and causality, thus preventing us from knowing the Ultimate Reality. This is why we must reduce the mind to silence, but we are hindered by the crystallized subconscious accumulations which the past has produced within us. These are the 'wandering spectres', the 'ghosts which smell of death', from which we must liberate ourselves by means of a 'rectification', which will give us the possibility of eliminating all that makes us slaves of the past, and of correcting those discordancies and disharmonies that have distorted the harmony of our rhythms.

The questions and answers come to an end with the exhortation to remember that we are the Absolute and with the mention of Art as being the means to the transformation of ideas into colours, words, sounds etc. The less they are qualified by the ego, the closer they will be to perfection.

We turn now to a blank page, as expressive and meaningful as if written. Here Raphael seems to say to the reader: Stop! So far I have answered your questions, and given you the possibility of transforming into knowledge that ignorance which is at the very basis of your questioning. But now stop, reflect, be silent, and in this empty silence, which is in front of you, meditate! Do not be in a hurry, and only when you seem to have understood what I have so far tried to impress on your heart, go on. And if you have also 'embraced' what you have understood, your knowledge will become consciousness.

The second part of the book is entitled the 'Pathway of Fire' and contains a series of *sūtras* or aphorisms, each of which is permeated by a vibrating and penetrating force which is far more than the beauty of its expression, for it aims to shake the reader out of his inertia and awaken him from his lethargy.

The 'Pathway of Fire' which, as Raphael shows us, is the 'Pathway' we need to follow in order to realize our own Essence, is the *path* which every disciple must pursue, whatever branch of the Tradition he belongs to. It is the Pathway of the 'Return'.[1]

The aphorisms are arranged in chapters, each of which has a basic theme. They may be defined as 'thoughts that vibrate'. As such, given a suitably conscious environment, they have the capacity to transcend the empirical, rational mind and go deep into the reader's consciousness. See, for example, aphorism 54, which seems to be the answer to the question with which the book opens: Does life really have a purpose?

Having listed with a dispassionate, objective and forceful examination the answers that man usually gives himself, and

---

[1] For a more complete exposition of the 'Pathway of Fire' in its alchemical, aesthetic and metaphysical aspects, refer to: Raphael, *The Threefold Pathway of Fire*, Aurea Vidyā, New York.

having shattered their credibility, Raphael presses on with other questions that move ever closer to the heart of the subject. Going beyond the pessimism of the questioner, he brings him to the recognition that if the struggle in which man is involved were directed only towards the transient, it would be a terrible hoax, 'a deception, and an irrational cruelty' (Aphorism 54). If life had no meaning that transcended the individual and his materiality, it would be truly absurd. In the first part the emphasis was laid so much on the transience of the physical body and of matter that in these aphorisms it becomes logical to deduce the true purpose of man's life, of this 'sleeping God', who has the freedom and the possibility of re-integrating himself into his own essence, where his existence is rooted (Aphorism 53). The possibility of creating his own destiny is in his own hands. He is the Demiurge. There is no God opposing the way his energies are directed. Thus each human being is given responsibility for his own actions, a responsibility which he has so self-indulgently delegated to God. It is so convenient to place one's responsibilities on someone else's shoulders! Here lies the danger of dualism, which can dull us with a false evaluation of our state of consciousness.

Thus, against modern man's anxious uncertainty, against his inner void filled only with confusion, loneliness, and fear, Raphael offers the firm safe rock of a valid reason for living and shows us that basing our life solely on physical materiality means losing contact with the Universal Reality, becoming a 'living corpse', and creating 'a society that is already dead'. The concept now expands into the social and political fields: in his work *Which Democracy?* Raphael clearly indicates the solution to these problems, which is briefly touched upon here, in a political system which is based on an ethical conduct that transcends individuality and is linked to universal laws.[1]

But in order to achieve this, man must examine himself and reveal the essence of his being. All that has been said in the answers about true love, the limitations of the mind, our position with regard to desire, the continuity of becoming, the need to liberate ourselves from the ego, from the memories of the past, from all dual and conflicting causes, from the powers of *māyā*, which withhold all possibility of transcendence, love and identity: all this now bears new fruit in the Aphorisms. Having cleared the points of greatest importance in the question and answer section and having insisted upon the necessity, or rather the duty, to undertake the journey towards realization with constancy, decision and courage, so that we may regain the 'solar power' which dissolves the lunar powers, Raphael, in a dizzying crescendo, deals with all the phases of the work of transformation which he expounds in terms taken from both Alchemy and the *Qabbālāh* (Aphorism 99-104).

These aphorisms describe a process of transformation from individuality to cosmic living, where the use of Fire is essential. In fact, all the Fires are indispensable for a gradual resolution of the world of object and the world of subject. One must abandon oneself to the All-pervading Fire which is Harmony, seize it from the 'Higher World', allow oneself to be burnt by it, merge all the Fires into a single Fire, and have the courage to watch it die out.

Raphael shows the reader, as well as the potential candidate for Realization, all the steps through which he must progress, all the difficulties he will meet and will have to overcome; he does not present the work that awaits him in an enticing form; on the contrary, he reveals its difficulties

---

[1] See Raphael, *The Philosophy of Being*. Aurea Vidyā, New York..

with the sureness of one who has experienced it all for himself. He warns the reader against superficial enthusiasm and the tricks of the mind. He hides nothing from him. He speaks to him of agony, of dying to himself, of the cross to which he must nail himself; it really cannot be said that the picture is inviting or that this 'Knower' of *Advaita* is looking for converts to *Asparśayoga*; in fact, it could be said that he is trying to drive them away.

Raphael understands that only those who possess the necessary qualifications can undertake this path, since there are other paths that are well-suited to people's different individual qualifications. Yet he continues to repeat that today it is imperative to 'transform oneself'.

In these aphorisms Raphael 'sounds' his note, and his cry provides a strong stimulus for those who, though having the appropriate qualifications, are still wasting time and dozing. This cry is for those who continue to nourish themselves on earthiness instead of devoting themselves to taming their horse and conquering themselves: 'If you wake up one morning determined to do something that you end up not doing, this means that you have not really woken up' (Aphorism 6).

One must not think that these aphorisms are lyrical flights of fancy expressed in a poetical form which is an end in itself. This is the style of pure metaphysical realization, which aims at teaching you to observe the dying out of the last central Fire into which all the others have dissolved. This is final, conclusive death in divine Solitude or in the 'flight of the solitary to the solitary'.

'This is the life of the gods and of men divine and blessed.
Detachment from all that remains below, life that takes no further delight in earthly things, flight of the solitary to the solitary.'[1]

The work has been completed and the human being, liberated from all that kept him on the plane of manifestation, has arrived 'at the springs of life', he has uncovered Being in itself and has found his identity with It: the human cycle is concluded.

Marina Zannelli.

---

[1] Plotinus, *Enneads* VI.9.11.

AT THE SOURCE OF LIFE

MAN'S IDEAL

Q[1]. I have always set ideals for myself, but sooner or later they have failed me. I am desperately seeking something that can give meaning to my life, but every time I look around me I see nothing but the ruins of these ideals. Today I am at the point of asking myself if there really is any purpose to life. What can you tell me about this?

R. Man wanders in the forest of becoming, riddled with doubt, conflict, and a sense of incompleteness. Throughout this entire process of loneliness and ignorance he tries to cling on to supports, which we call ideals. But after some time he is obliged to surrender because, in fact, the true purpose of existence has escaped him. What might this purpose be?

Q. That of understanding oneself, I think.

R. What do we mean by understanding? Please let us try to grasp this concept together, otherwise our exchange will be a mere drawing-room conversation and not a dialogue leading to realization. If a person is told that the

---

[1] Q = Question.
R = Raphael.
− = The same person who asked the previous question.

road he is taking has no exit, and that, in order to reach his destination he must take the opposite direction, and that person says he has understood and yet continues down the same dead-end, this means that that person has not really *understood*.

To understand means to 'take a datum within oneself', to integrate its conceptual contents, to penetrate the essence of the thing.

Therefore, if we understand our true Essence, we cannot but be that Essence in every place, time and causality.

Q. This act of self-understanding requires time, withdrawal from the world, and solitude. I go to work every day and I find myself in this frantic world; how can I reach such a favourable state?

R. To understand ourselves do we really have to retire into the jungle or to the top of a mountain? Whether we are in the city, in the country or elsewhere, wherever we go we take our conflict and our incompleteness with us.

We could be in the mountains, surrounded by solitude, and have a restless mind and find anything but silence. On the other hand, the opposite could happen to us in the city. Withdrawing is a state of mind. Self-understanding does not depend on place or time. The ego, alas, always tries to avoid the basic problem.

Can we understand ourselves when we are weighed down by work? Who is it that is working? What relationship is there between us and our work? What is work? Can we work while being somewhere else with our minds? While we are walking, for example, can we think of some other event?

To discover all of this means to understand ourselves, and we can realize this process in any psycho-physical condition, whatever it may be.

Q. I always thought that man's ideal must be that of loving his neighbour. Do you think that there can be a higher ideal?

R. It would require far more time to answer this question fully. However, I shall try as far as I can to clarify the problem. First of all, I would like to ask you what you mean by love? We must begin from a clear and precise point, otherwise we shall never be able to... understand each other.

– (After some hesitation) To be useful to others, to serve others, and not to fight each other. All this, in my view, means love.

R. Then, one must serve and be useful to others. But this requires some knowledge, as well as maturity on the part of the giver, don't you agree? Can the blind ever lead the blind?

– Certainly not.

R. One who gives *must* have, one who wants to teach *must* know, one who wants to love others *must* possess love. Otherwise, what does one give?
You nod, but perhaps you are not following me adequately. Do all of you follow me? The problem is delicate and demanding. Let us create the right kind of attention without any subconscious resistance. In this way we can discover unusual things together.

— I see there are many implications in my question...

R. That is not important: the issue has been raised. Let us go as far as we can. Let us take an example: what must a potential teacher do if he wants to instruct others, and thus serve and love them?

— First of all, he must have knowledge.

R. That is correct. So let us say that he must reach a true understanding of things, which, in turn, will cause a qualitative 'outpouring' and an 'irradiation', which may take the form of a pedagogical gift or something else. Or, rather, we can say that the act of love matures when true understanding is alive in us. To understand means to love, to give, to share, isn't that so? Man's ideal consists in realizing oneself, in living the true principial Essence; all the rest is a logical consequence. The flower that has reached maturity cannot but give out its perfume, so that all those who approach it can experience its fragrance and the beauty of its geometry. An Awakened Being is Beauty, Perfume, and Geometry, and by its presence alone that Being imposes a rhythm on space. This condition is non-dual.

TRUE LOVE

Q. What does this last statement mean?

R. It means that true love is neither emotional nor sexual, because these imply exclusive, conflicting desire, possession and some kind of *return*.

Q. Does that love we were talking about before not imply duality just the same; must there not be two people involved in any case?

R. Let us return to the state of free attention. These nuances are so subtle we cannot let the mind wander.
When I say that a flower irradiates its perfume, the quality of the perfume reveals itself independently of the existence of people or things on the outside. The sun gives its light regardless of the existence of the planets. In this action there is no appropriation, desire, slavery, no memory, and no duality; do you understand? Patañjali calls this state kaivalya, isolation from all duality, divine Solitude.[1] This implies irradiating, giving without receiving, without any form of return. Where there is desire, there is always duality and conflict, and therefore incompleteness. We have,

---

[1] See Patāñjali, *Yogadarśana* (The Regal Way to Realization). By Raphael. Aurea Vidyā, New York.

more or less, mistaken desire for love. The ego always desires: cars, sex, positions of power, even paradise itself, but it desires just to obtain enjoyment, to achieve emotional tranquillity, to gratify its subconscious greed.

– So, if I love someone I must expect nothing? Must I let that person go?

R. It seems obvious to me; if there is pure love, then there can never be any kind of requirement; if, on the other hand, there is desire, then things are very different.
Try to reflect, please. We are here to understand each other, and therefore to love each other.
Can light desire light, being itself light?
Can knowledge desire knowledge, being itself knowledge?
Can life desire life, being itself life?
Can love desire love, being itself love?

– All this is marvellous; at the same time, it is terrible, at least for me, to recognize certain patterns of human behaviour and certain human impulses.

R. You must not let that sadden you; if he is to reach his goal, his genuine Ideal - Realization of the Essence -, a person must have the courage to come to terms with his inner enemies.

MAN'S ENEMY

Q. What is man's worst enemy?

R. Ignorance.

Q. How can we defeat it? Can you show us a way?

R. Only by means of Realization, by reawakening oneself to what in reality one is, which entails the kind of understanding we spoke of earlier.

Q. How can we obtain this Realization?

R. It is not a question of acquiring, gaining or obtaining some thing. In reality, we can never acquire anything that we do not potentially possess. Potentially we are realized already, and we only have to demonstrate this at the conscious level.

Q. The *Vedānta*[1] path, which I value very much, states that we are *Brahman* but that we do not recognize ourselves as such because *māyā* is interposed between us and It. How can I eliminate this veil which prevents me from seeing myself for what I really am?

---
[1] See Raphael, *The Pathway of Non-Duality*, Aurea Vidyā, New York.

R. With the sword of discrimination and with the light of illumination which results from it. You must separate the Real from the unreal, the Self from non-Self, true Knowledge from erudite cognition and from accumulation, the Noumenon from phenomenon, and the Self from the vehicular compound or the instrument of contact.

Let us first of all recognize the fact that we are the Self, or, to speak in Western terms, a Spark of God. We must recover this principial condition of ours. Metaphysical ignorance has darkened our consciousness, but this ignorance is merely a ghost which comes and goes and which can be destroyed. It depends on the direction we want to give our minds. Śaṅkara states that the mind has brought us to slavery, but that the mind itself will also lead us to Liberation.[1]

Q. It happens that, although the mind understands the need to follow a certain line, it refuses to do so. Why does this happen?

R. The mind is weighed down by memories, by its past, by what it has learnt, by inhibitions, by fear, by doubts and so on. The contents of the mind constitute our fatal incompleteness. How can we cleanse the mind of this waste material? How can we dispel the subconscious ghosts that suck our blood and impoverish us day in and day out? This is the problem.

Q. Can the mind recognize all this incompleteness, being itself incomplete?

---

[1] For further insights on the subject refer to *Dṛigdṛśyaviveka*, attributed to Śaṅkara; and Śaṅkara, *Vivekacūḍāmaṇi*. Translation from Sanskrit and commentary by Raphael. Aurea Vidyā, New York.

R. You must discover that for yourself. Take envy, for example. Try to trace the movement of the energy involved in yourself: when it is born, why it is born, how it matures, and how it urges you to behave in a certain manner. Follow this process of incompleteness from birth to maturity and then its consequent outward expression. You must make envy into an *object* of knowledge; this implies the presence of an acting subject. If we were only mind we would never be able to realize ourselves. Fortunately, the mind is only a tool, the reflection of something that lies behind it.

– Envy stems from an external object.

R. I don't think so. Envy stems from your internal reaction, as an answer to an external object. Don't you agree?

Different people react in different ways to the same object. This shows that the object has nothing at all to do with it. On the contrary, what appears fundamental is your response, your reaction to it. If we want to understand ourselves, we must move our gaze away from the external world and turn it towards the furnace of our inner reactive impulses. Our enemies are within and not without.

– This really opens up new horizons for me. Excuse me for making the following consideration: based on what we have said, it seems that what produces a certain kind of restlessness in me is not somebody's behaviour but my inner response or reaction to it. Is that so? I would like to grasp this better. I am here to try to understand.

R. I think that this process should be quite clear. We do not depend on external behaviour or objects, but on our own reactions to them. What is needed is to re-educate these very reactions, and not the external objects or events.

– So the way in which we condemn today's consumer society is wrong. If we should condemn something, shouldn't it be our own particular reaction to it?

R. Yes. Consumer goods are simply innocent instruments of service; it depends on us whether we allow ourselves to be more or less enslaved by them.

Q. So it is necessary to reverse today's morality. Don't you think that man blames his weakness or, as you call it, his *incompleteness*, on external factors?

R. I agree. This is why Realization is difficult at times. The ego never wants to recognize itself for what it is. Considerable attention is needed for an understanding, as well as great humility and an intelligent attitude of acceptance. Our past and all that we have learned needs to be wiped clean, like a *tabula rasa* (clean slate). The ego is always looking for new sensations, in meditation and outside of meditation; it seeks mystery, not truth, because truth can reveal some rather unpleasant things to the ego.

THE LIMITS OF THE MIND

Q. Can the mind comprehend the Absolute or *Brahman*? Can intellectual knowledge penetrate the mystery of Being?

R. The mind, as we have said, is a perceptive tool similar to the physical one. It is a simple vehicle thanks to which the entity comes into contact with certain possibilities of being. Like all vehicles or tools for making contact, it is limited and contingent. It apprehends truth, let us say, indirectly. This implies that it compares, selects and then comes to conclusions that are obviously not absolute, nor can they be.

After all, we are aware of the imprecision of the mind, and to compensate for this deficiency we have tried to create logical systems and forms of analogical, syllogistic reasoning etc., based on certain inductive or deductive premises. But such systems are the products of that same conditioned mind; therefore they cannot be considered absolutes.

Science itself must continually modify the concepts it previously considered valid. The form or image of a nineteenth-century physicist is not the same as that of today's atomic physicist. In universal life there are different planes of manifestation and of consciousness. Man possesses different 'windows'; each one of them is capable of making contact with a particular existential plane. Physiological sight for example, is useful only if a certain kind of environment exists. If light were to disappear, the eye's retina would no longer register anything. Now, the mind grasps perceptions by analysing them, comparing them and conceptualizing them, but it remains within the ambit of the sensory, of the dual, of the fragmentary, of time and of causality.

Besides, it observes only data external to itself; that is to say, it turns everything into an *object* of perception. But how can we comprehend the knowing subject? If we rely again on our mind, it will automatically turn the subject that we wish to know into an object, and this object once again presupposes a knowing subject.

In this process the mind *projects* a form or image of the real subject and it is on that form or image that it determines its thinking process. This means that it does not operate on the *thing in itself* but on the projection of its own imagination. Thus, we have an interpretation of the universe according to our mental form or image and not according to its intrinsic reality.

A Hindu proverb says that we cannot dance on our own shoulders. In the same way, the mind cannot comprehend itself. Thus we can observe the limits of a cognitive tool and acknowledge this observation with humility and acceptance. But the mind, which produces the ego, time, space and causality, will not surrender and, in its ignorant movement, will attempt to define, conceptualize, and grasp what is timeless, causeless, spaceless; in short, the mind is not self-illuminating or self-knowing. Something exists behind it, from which it draws a modest cognitive reflection. We can compare this something to the sun, which shines with its own light.

The task of the realization process is that of drawing consciousness back into this central Sun, which does not need any mind or thought to understand because It comprehends the all and comprehends Itself. If this central Self is compared to the sun and the mind to the moon, what is the use of the moon's pale reflection when the sun shines at its zenith?[1]

Q. If the mind is an impediment to the knowledge of the *ātman*, how can I overcome it?

R. The mind can constitute an obstacle only when it insists on exercising a prerogative which does not belong to it. If it manages to appreciate its own limits by means of supra-mental illumination, it can be of valid assistance, just as other vehicles are.

Q. Then is it not a question of bringing it back to its proper dimension, of giving it its proper place and its proper function?

R. Yes. One must give the mind its proper dimension, which is measure, then bring it to active silence. In such mental solitude the Unknown will emerge.

Q. How can the mind be brought back to its proper dimension if it is the cause of deceit?

R. We are going around the same problem in a circle. Let us try to get out of this circle. The fact that we can consciously formulate, direct, or inhibit thought means that we are not mind or thought. If you are capable of making the statements you have made here, it means that there is a centre behind the mind that can intervene and watch the passage of mental images or ideas. On the other hand, one

---

[1] See also, Raphael, *Tat tvam asi*, That thou art, Aurea Vidyā, New York.

needs to experience that condition in which one remains without thought and without images.

Q. I have experienced that condition and I recognize its validity, but I would like to understand more thoroughly the mechanism that unfortunately pulls me out of that condition of absence of thought. In short, what is it which urges me to come out of that, let us call it, position of quiet, silence, and solitude?

R. To understand this event we must first of all examine the thinking process in its dynamics, and then work our way back to the cause that incites the mind to produce an image or idea. The mind is a maker and at the same time a recorder of images; it is unable to think other than with *ideal models*; a pure abstraction is, in fact, unthinkable. Thus we can compare it to a film on which images and entire thought sequences are formed. In his *Yoga Sūtra*, Patañjali says that the mind takes on the form of the object which is thought of or perceived and in turn the subject takes on the functions of the mind. We therefore have the subject identifying with the form or image which the mind projects, while in turn the mind becomes the perceived object. All of this is a mental game.

I would like you to please follow this process with the greatest attention, for we could make some interesting discoveries. Let us give an example. The mind of an actor projects the image of Julius Caesar (whose part he is playing), and the ego or actor identifies himself with this mental image to such an extent that he says: 'I am Julius Caesar'. This creates a scission between the true entity and what we may call the illusory entity. As long as the division lasts we find ourselves in the existential condition of... dreaming.

It is from this very condition that we must awaken. Those who are truly awakened are those who have solved all divisions and have discovered themselves as unconditioned. Therefore, on the backdrop of the Absolute within us we have superimposed a series of images and non-realities to the point where we mistake these dream images for the Absolute.

This is what Śaṅkara means when he states that we mistake a rope for a snake. The snake is simply our thought modification, a harmless image or projection with which the ego merges by falling into *avidyā* or ignorance. This is not the place to go into details on how the mind reproduces the objective forms or the endless variety of sensory perceptions as images.

Now, if we recall the mental film we spoke about before, which takes us continually into the world of becoming, we shall discover that there is a hiatus, a gap between one perception and the next, just as there is gap between one frame of the film and the next or, as science itself has discovered, between one photon of light and the next. That the universe was a continuum-discontinuum has been known to *Vedānta* metaphysics for a long time.

Yoga Vedānta meditation leads to a slowing down of the imagining or thinking sequence until one enters into that unmanifest *continuum* which is true Reality and which is not subject to change. We must discover what this Reality or Void, this divine Silence, this non-objectifying, non-projecting possibility is. Any kind of intellectual speculation would be vain, because thought would simply create other illusory images, other conceptualizations capable of satisfying only the *mentalists*.

Let us now take a look at the second part of the question.

What is that which takes us back to becoming? I think this is the question.

If we have experienced, I will not say the ultimate phase of the *samādhi* process – because the condition (which is a non-condition) of which we spoke a moment ago is a proper type of *samādhi* – but at least the condition of self-presence or the condition of observer, as soon as stillness of mind was achieved, we noticed that the mind found itself in a thought vortex because overwhelming images or forms entered our mental space. We may say that the energetic dynamism of *stored* images is strongly conditioning us considerably. Only one who has experienced this meditative process can recognize the real nature of psychical contents, their potent dynamism, and their irresistible conditioning power is. What is required of the true aspirant to Realization is to free himself from this past, from this accumulation, from these wandering apparitions, and from these phantoms which reek of death.

So every time we try to bring silence to our minds, this dynamism urges us to express ourselves outwardly. And one must be very careful, because *inhibiting* the mind is of no use; on the contrary, it produces the opposite effect. Mental silence is not the result of inhibition, but of the *solution*[1] of the entire imprisoning, energetic accumulation.

Thus there are two factors that induce the mind to form dreams and images: the first factor is the product of our immense resource of subconscious energy which is filled with crystallized ideals demanding satisfaction; the second factor is produced by the habit of the extroverted, uncontrolled mind which models itself on the various perceptions by solidifying them.

---

[1] Solution: 1. the action or process of solving; the state, condition, or fact of being solved.
To solve: 4. to dissolve, put an end to. 5. to dissolve, to melt.
The Shorter Oxford English Dictionary, vol. II. Clarendon Press, Oxford.

The control of the mind's inclination towards an objectifying extroversion and the *solution* of the subconscious powers are the two most important pillars of the *Yogadarśana* training.

Q. Can psychoanalysis solve these problems?

R. Psychoanalysis does not resolve but supports the subconscious issue. This is the difference between the *yogi* and the psychoanalyst; the latter operates at the level of individuality, working on issues of the conflicting ego, while the former, on the contrary, operates to resolve and transcend the whole of human individuality. There is no opposition between the two, but the methods and the goals differ, and so it is best to avoid all comparisons.

* * *

R. Let us resume the dialogue of the other evening and try, as is our practice, to foster the appropriate level of attention which can take us into the world of meaning. There are new faces here this evening; I have been told, however, that many of them have listened to the recording. We can therefore continue with the questions.

Q. I heard the recording of the other evening and found the solution to some of my doubts as a disciple, but I did not understand the difference between mind, thought, ideas etc. What am I to resolve? The mind, thoughts, or something else? The answer to this question is very important for me.

R. When we speak of vehicles, or sheaths, we refer to that energy compound which is kept in a certain form by the vital strength of an inner Centre. When this Centre withdraws its cohesive strength from a vehicle, the vehicle disintegrates and disperses into space. We can observe this process when we witness the end of the gross body we wear. Every vehicle expresses certain qualities and characteristics that are inherent in its nature.

Thus the mental vehicle is an energy compound that responds to certain possibilities; we may say that it is sensitive to the world of perceptions, ideas, and concepts. The mind has the ability to visualize or project entire universes and perceive them simultaneously.

What conditions that vehicle is the *solidifying* energy of the images and ideas. A mental image is charged with energy; it constitutes a life potential which, sooner or later, must find an outlet, or otherwise it changes into tension. A mental content is like a Leyden jar: it may explode in our psyche[1] at any moment. When unresolved, it is a psychic tumour which produces perturbation and conflict. So it is not the mental vehicle as such that we must destroy, but the fossilized products stagnating within its ambit, which are conditioning and poisoning it.

Just as the physical body produces certain crystallizations which in time become refuse and must be eliminated to prevent blood poisoning, so the mind produces certain conceptual, ideal crystallizations that must be eliminated if one wants to avoid mental illness.

Unfortunately, the individual is strongly attached to his own mental contents that he creates truly abnormal states

---

[1] Psyche: the animating principle in man and other living beings, the source of all vital activities, rational or irrational, the soul or spirit, in distinction to its material vehicle; sometimes considered as capable of persisting in a disembodied state after separation from the body at death.

1. The soul, or spirit, as distinguished from the body; the mind.
The Shorter Oxford English Dictionary, vol. II. Op. cit.

or severe conflict. He is never the person of today, of the present; he is always the person of the past, of his memory, living in the stench of his own putrefied psychical corpses. The consciousness of the human being is torn between the critical weight of millions of dead, solidified days and the present moment which is its real existential condition.

Q. Is this a kind of purification at a deep level?

R. Exactly. *Vedānta* poses the problem of purification in terms of vibration. Let me explain. A psychical[1] content of pride or of sense of separateness produces a certain vibratory state in us which, in turn, becomes attuned to other similar states and thus increases. We attract vibrations corresponding to our state. Our hatred attracts hatred, our pride attracts pride, and so on. If we want to break this vicious circle of squalor we must learn how to vibrate so as to touch those upper harmonics that transcend our egoistical human condition. All this constitutes a deep alchemical process, and means operating with intelligence as well as with an understanding of the laws of vibration. In fact, there is no idea, concept, or content of consciousness that is not the result of some vibratory energy.

Ideas travel on harmonics of light. Words are vibrating substances. An entity, whatever dimension it may belong to, is a vibrating mode of consciousness; every form is an energetic effect or movement, a rhythm, and a symphony of light waves.

A mineral, a vegetable, an animal, a star, a lovely face or a beautiful flower, a smile or a child's glance: all of these are simply harmonies of rhythms. Perfect vibratory measure

---

[1] Psychic: of or pertaining to the human soul or mind; mental: psychical. The Shorter Oxford English Dictionary, vol. II. Op. cit.

produces harmony. As we can see, we cannot cause love to emerge simply by pronouncing the word 'love': first of all, we must evoke in ourselves an adequate rhythm or a responsive harmonic state. To purify means to eliminate all discordant vibrations. It is not a moralistic question, but one of harmonising oneself with the universal sound of Being.[1]

---

[1] For this aspect of harmony, see Chapter 'Vibrating life' in *Beyond Doubt* by Raphael. Aurea Vidyā, New York.

WE ARE THE CHILDREN OF DESIRE

Q. I ask myself why I am here. Can you tell me?

R. I think you are referring to this plane of existence. Let us discuss this question together.

In re-examining your past life you may ask yourself: what was it that induced me to follow a given line and urged me into action?

— I find it difficult to say at the moment.

R. I'll help you. What is your job?

— I work in an office...

R. Good! Was there ever a time when you wanted to be, let's say, somebody in your own field?

— To tell you the truth, I began my job with a legitimate desire to make a success of my career or — as they say — to get ahead.

R. So at that time you lived to satisfy a desire, to crown a dream, to gratify an ideal.

— Certainly, I used to live for that.

R. So, at a certain time, you were urged to move, pressed by a particular need for power, for vanity, for economic improvement, etc. Let us now take another phase in your life. Which one could it be?... Do you have a family?

— Yes. I am married and we have two children.

R. So here we have another period characterized by desire, this time for a family, for a companion, for children etc.; a desire to overcome loneliness. This represents the gratification of a need for appropriation, sensation, and ego-centred satisfaction. We could continue but we will stop here.

Then, why do we live this planetary condition of consciousness? To satisfy our sensory needs, to crown certain ideals, to enjoy material, intellectual, spiritual benefits; we are here to express our thirst for pride, vanity, power, etc. You are here to satisfy countless desires, whether good or bad, elevated or base, altruistic or selfish and so on. We are the children of desire, and only the cessation of desire can liberate us.

— But is it possible to live without desires?

R. I could answer, 'All you have to do is to try it.' After all, Realization is not mere discursiveness. On the other hand, we could ask ourselves whether there is a mode of consciousness without desire, a condition of Completeness, Absoluteness, Joy without an object, and movement around our own axis, or whether we are destined to live forever in conflict and pain without escape.

Q. I have noticed that desire is always dualistic.

R. Wherever there is desire there is also the object of desire, an orbital movement around a datum or event; but duality is incompleteness.

— Did Buddha in his sermons refer to what we are saying?

R. The predominant questions in the East are: What are human sufferings and conflicts? What is the origin of this conflict and disharmony? How can this conflict be eliminated? How should we live in order to be in harmony with ourselves, our fellow humans and with nature itself?
Finding the answer to these questions means solving the problem of the individual, and living a philosophy of life; and being in line with this philosophy in practical life means Realizing oneself.
Eastern philosophy is of a practical, empirical nature; the process leading to realization is both practical and empirical; the outcome is metaphysics.
Buddha, with his Illumination, discovered that the life of becoming is permeated with conflict and pain. The Four Noble Truths deal with suffering, the origin of suffering, the ceasing of suffering, and the way that leads to the solution of suffering or conflict. According to Buddha, thirst for pleasure or enjoyment, desire to be *this* or *that*, and desire for certain dual experiences constitute the origin of suffering. *Nirvana* represents *Pax profunda*, Completeness, Fullness, rotating on one's own axis, and Joy without desire. But in *nirvana*, obviously, that empirical, grasping and selfish ego no longer exists: only the Self or Life as such exists, without definitions or qualifications.
Did not Christ Himself reveal Love that is Joy without desire?

Q. Does joy not exist in us, then?

R. If suffering exists, then joy must exist too. It is up to you to discover where and how to find one or the other.

— There is no need to discover pain; unfortunately one sees it so often...

R. As far as joy is concerned, however, you seem uncertain, you do not know where to find it nor how to hold on to it. Is that not so?

— I have experienced it at times. But so rarely!

R. And it probably was simply sensory joy produced by the satisfaction of some desire. When we enjoy ourselves we are happy; but this is not the type of happiness I mean, this is sensory and fleeting happiness. I am speaking of Joy without desire.

— Can you give me an example?

R. Please, let us hold the proper kind of attention. Here on the table you can see my briefcase. At the moment I think that you feel no desire for it. You see it, you can touch it, but you receive no stimulus from it that can *modify your consciousness*. In short, there is no reaction in you; you are satisfied with your present vibratory state; you are not leaving your psychical space in order to produce action, orbital movement, or change of thought. We can say that you live in your own fullness as far as that object is concerned. Is that not so?

– Certainly. It cannot condition my consciousness either by attraction or repulsion; I feel nothing; I am indifferent.

R. So, although you are faced with an object, you remain in the deepest state of peace, in 'divine indifference'. Extend this condition to all the objects which our planetary material life can offer, including envy, competitiveness, distinction, etc.

– Is this the condition of the Liberated?

R. Just as there are elementary particles (for example, neutrinos) that enter and emerge from the electromagnetic field of the atom without undergoing any kind of transformation –neither attraction nor repulsion – there are also personalities that enter into and emerge from the human electromagnetic field without undergoing alterations. These individuals are called the Liberated, the Awakened, the living Realized, or *jīvanmukta*, to use the *Vedānta* term.

Q. In order to be liberated must one simply eliminate every desire?

R. You talk as if detachment from the world of the ego and all its attributes is easy.

Q. You claim that by killing all desire one gets liberated. I think that this surgical operation is truly effective. In other words, it is like amputating a leg to free a patient from conflict and pain.

R. Do you recognize in desire the cause of human conflict, not to be able to get what one wants?

— What one is interested in.

R. Interest in something, desire, interest, or feeling in order to obtain material, intellectual, spiritual objects and events. Desires are externalized in thousands of ways, from that simple, basic, childlike desire for a toy to that refined one for wealth, or even spiritual riches.

Do you not agree that, if this cause ceased, conflict, suffering and duality would also cease?

— And how can I eliminate desire?

R. Shall we examine this problem together? We could inhibit it, and this would be the amputation you talked about. It is well known by now that inhibition cannot solve the problem and, on the other hand, as long as the *roots* of desire exist, inhibition is nonsensical. We could also eliminate, or get rid of, all the objects that arouse desires, so that, being deprived of external stimulation, they could not express themselves. This, however, would simply be another kind of inhibition, a violent operation not on the subject but on the object. As we have already seen, it is neither the external nor the internal objects that condition us, but our *response*, our *reaction* to them. There is another way: that of inhibiting thought, so that, because we are no longer thinking, desire or emotion would no longer be perceived at the conscious level. But this is a temporary solution because when thought returns, then emotion too surfaces again.

Then we have the evasion based on various sports, sex, amusement, or involvement in pious and meritorious activities, going here and there to preach the word of one's own evasion and incompleteness.

We must not inhibit, kill or avoid desire. Nor should we, on the other hand, silence it or offer it more or less innocent or morally wholesome outlets; we must, instead, *resolve* desire. As you can see, the problem is quite different.

To resolve any problem means eliminating the problem itself. Now we know that a datum can be resolved in one way only: by comprehending it. Is that not so? When we comprehend desire, when we trace this energy that emerges, advances and forces us into conflict, when we comprehend its true movement we find ourselves freed from limitation and slavery, and where there is comprehension there cannot be inhibition, flight or anything else.

– Do you think that by comprehending desire we have the solution to the human problem?

R. My brother, it is by comprehending our own movement that we can transcend ourselves. By comprehending the origin of conflict and therefore of duality we can, in the end, find our Completeness.

– Do I need a Teacher to comprehend myself?

R. One only needs a heart that is able to reveal itself, a heart that has ceased to desire even the most beautiful, spiritual, or elevated things, a heart that has recovered Quietness without an object. Any human being can be of great help to another, but the true solution to our lack of completeness is for us alone to tackle and realize.

– This comprehension, how can we achieve it?

R. By means of discrimination between real and unreal, noumenon and phenomenon, Self and non-Self. The way of the *jñāni*, however, is not made up of simple philosophical deductions and inductions. These only represent a cognitive way by which the conceptual and phenomenal superimpositions hiding Reality are eliminated.

Q. In other words, by eliminating that idea of the snake superimposed on the rope?

R. Śaṅkara, in fact, offers this example to give us a better understanding of this projecting mechanism of the mind. We have seen that already.

* * *

R. Let us resume this cycle of conversations in the hope that it may lead to a greater understanding of ourselves.

We should keep in mind the fact that ours are stimulating conversations which require a conscious attention and intuitive penetration which, in turn, may reveal the truth dwelling in the depth of our hearts.

Personally, I am not the depository of Truth; nor do I dare place myself in a missionary or apostolic position. Truth requires no advocates. Truth is there, has always been there and always will be everywhere and at all times. It reveals itself by itself when proper discrimination and intelligent reflection are active. Truth cannot be locked into a scheme, a teaching, or a philosophical 'system', nor can it be given as if it were a box of sweets; yet it offers itself to those who are capable of *loving it*. But human beings do not love Truth; instead they love the erudition of the mind, and their ego with all its varied contents, or life in all its changing and fluctuating forms, with the glory of material and spiritual powers, and their own salvation, as long as it is effected and granted by others.

When we understand that Truth is not our past, made up of pride, haughtiness, separateness, selfishness, or worldly and spiritual cravings, when we discover that Truth is something Innocent, Essential and Simple, which resides in all the expressions of life, then, with great humility, we shall know how to banish all that our mind has accumulated up to now.

Love reveals reality and reality is permeated by love; to comprehend is to love, and love is found in those who are pure of heart, in those who turn to Life and not toward objects which bind us and make us greedy slaves.

REALITY, THE ABSOLUTE

Q. We have often spoken of the Absolute, of reality, of truth; but what is reality after all?

R. I see that you go right to the heart of the matter, but is this simple curiosity or is it a request coming from the very depth of your being? Mere curiosity has never revealed the mysteries of life.

– No, it's not curiosity. I have always asked myself what reality is, but I have never found it or discovered it among the many books, even those of a spiritual nature, which I have read. Perhaps I haven't looked in the right direction.

R. If you seek erudition in the boundless ways of the world of names and forms, then read certain books. There are many of them that are very interesting and well documented. They are not to be disregarded or ignored. They explain the multiplicity of the life of the forms on each manifest plane, what the beings of a lower, upper or divine kind are, the chain of cosmic energies and the possibility of coming into contact with them. But Reality is not all this; It stands behind this entire scenario, this grandiose show of life. It is not written in books, but is revealed by those hearts that are capable of questioning and comprehending themselves. Reality is not an idea, a concept or a moral proposition; it cannot be perceived by the sense of hearing or by the retina of the eye.

Let us establish certain basic principles so that we can discover something stimulating.

I will now read some thoughts of Max Planck, Nobel Prize winner for physics:

'In the first paragraph of this autobiographical outline, I emphasized the fact that for me the quest for something *absolute* is the noblest and most worthy purpose of science. The reader may well consider my overt interest in the theory of relativity as a contradiction. But it would be a fundamental error to consider things in this way because all that is relative presupposes something *absolute* and has meaning only when compared with something *absolute*. The usual expression 'all is relative' is ambiguous and without sense. Even the theory of relativity itself is based on something *absolute*, that is the metric determination of the time-space continuum; the quest for the absolute is a particularly important task, as it alone can give some sense to something relative. All our measurements are relative. The matter of which our instruments are made varies depending on its geographical origins, their construction depends on the skill of the designer and the maker; their application is contingent upon the aims pursued by the researcher. Our task is to find in all of these factors and data *the absolute, the universally valid, the unvarying hidden in them*.'[1]

This concept is metaphysical in its essence and this evening we will try to look more deeply into it. When we speak of the Real we identify it, without even noticing it, with 'something' absolute, eternally valid, independent of any

---

[1] Max Planck, *Scientific Autobiography*. Einaudi, Turin, Italy 1954. [The italics are ours].

determination, something that need not depend on anything but itself. If a datum is absolute it must have autonomous life unto itself, an intrinsic existence regardless of any other datum. Given what we have considered, whether other data exist or not is of no importance whatsoever, because this datum exists rightly as an independent, unchanging reality which we might well call Absolute.

If, on the other hand, this datum of ours does not enjoy autonomous, intrinsic, unchanging existence, it means that its existence is subordinate to another datum which provides it with life and a name. In this case the datum is not absolute Reality because it has proven simply to be a relative, contingent, transitory phenomenon.

Reality is such if it does not depend on any other reality. If we hold this statement to be valid, then, with the sword of discernment, we can reject whatever does not correspond to it. The Vedantic *'neti, neti'* (not this, not this) refers precisely to this way of proceeding. Thus, first of all, we have an awareness of an 'absolute value', then a cognitive discernment which permits us to discard whatever does not correspond to this value, and finally a proceeding towards or, rather, a *falling* into *That*, whose nature is Silence. All forms of cosmogony refer to objective manifestation, to a substantial datum, to the world of names and forms, as we have already suggested, whereas metaphysics refers to the Essence, the unvarying Absolute, or the Principle without beginning or end, which, therefore, is beyond time and space, and outside all duality. It is important to keep this distinction in mind because some teachings deal with manifestation (the world of names and forms), while others dare to go beyond, and transcend manifestation. This has often led to considerable incomprehension and to useless and childish arguments between the supporters of these two points of view. In any case, having reached the plane of *kaivalya*, which is all-encompassing Silence, the Realized man has transcended both teachings.

What, then, is Reality? As it cannot be thought – otherwise we would simply create a mental image of reality – it must be realized, and to realize it we need to transform ourselves and examine in depth the value of our perception. By eliminating whatever is not reality from the field of our consciousness, we shall understand what Reality is and only thus shall we be Reality.[1]

– How can I consider myself Absolute if I am relative?

R. Do you consider your relativity absolute or relative? If it is absolute, we are faced with two absolutes; if it is relative, it must depend on something else which, obviously, you must look for and demonstrate.

– Let me clarify what I mean: it seems inconceivable to the mind that I should be an absolute.

R. It could not be otherwise because the mind is relative. If you question your mind you will come to the conclusion that you are contingent, but if you ask your Heart you will obtain the opposite answer. All humanity behaves as if it were to live forever, and this is caused by a deep and unconscious yearning for the absolute.

Q. According to our definition of the Real or absolute, I must conclude that everything around me is merely relative. Therefore I ask myself: for what reason do I live this unreal

---

[1] See also the chapter 'What is Intended by Reality' in Raphael, *Tat tvam asi*, That thou art. Op. cit.; Gauḍapāda, *Māṇḍūkyakārikā*, by Raphael. Aurea Vidyā, New York.

life, with my work and my family? And if everybody were to abandon this life, what would become of the planet?

R. To the first part of the question we can answer that wherever there is superimposition, change, birth, development, maturity and death, there is incompleteness, phenomenon, relativity and conflict. This is experiential evidence.

The second part of the question is not formulated correctly. Truth does not take the problem of the empirical ego and its particular sphere of existence into consideration.

Q. Can I experience the relative without entering into conflict? Is this possible?

R. Let us make it clear that the relative is such if compared to the ultimate Reality. Conflict arises only when we consider the relative to be absolute and identify with it. In other words, we mistake the rope for the snake. We turn our backs to the Light and perceive only the shadows of objects, considering them actual reality. This is also Plato's idea.[1] Identification with what is not, sooner or later leads to conflict.

Q. Why this contrast between the relative and the absolute? Is this not yet another duality to be overcome?

R. Duality exists when we want to make the relative absolute, as we usually do when we take the empirical point of view. If we state that a datum is relative, this means that we are faced with a simple phenomenon which is not

---

[1] See also the chapter 'Platonic ascent' in Raphael, *Initiation into the Philosophy of Plato*. Aurea Vidyā, New York.

absolute. When you dream you simply project relative data which disappear as soon as you wake up. The dream is superimposed on your reality as Being, but the latter is no dream. Being is permanent, the dreamer existed before the dream and goes on existing after it. The world of names and forms is born, grows and vanishes, but the Absolute, the Unchanging, the Constant, That which has neither birth nor death, does not vanish. Reality is beyond all duality.

Q. Is the life we live simply a dream then?

R. For those who identify with it, it cannot be a dream. Our dream at night is real enough to make us suffer, be happy, act, become enthusiastic, hate and love; so how can it be an illusion? Only when you awake, and look *from the point of view of wakefulness*, will you notice that you have dreamt, and not before.

– So I am dreaming even when I'm awake but do not know it, is that what you mean? This is all new to me, even amusing, but at the same time worrying and dramatic.

R. What have you done until now but pursue dreams and ideals? As a young man you did nothing but dream and imagine being 'this' or 'that'; today you have already lived out a large part of this dream and later you will certainly be obliged to abandon it. Every human being is playing his more or less humble role as projected by his mental powers. When on the stage of life the whole series of 'roles' is over, we have the Awakened man. He has at last discovered the truth concerning the play, the spectator, and the actor.

I would like to emphasize yet again the fact that the whole of empirical life constitutes a simple dream-super-imposition *only* when observed from an ontological point of view; in the same way, the dream at night is such *only* if considered from the point of view of wakefulness.

Q. Isn't every perception of ours a reality? If I perceive this chair near me, is it a dream? Isn't everything science discovers real?

R. Even in your dream you perceive the chair, and while you use it in your dream that chair is undoubtedly real. In the same way, your waking perception of the chair is real. But sensory perception in itself has nothing definite, complete or absolute.

Furthermore, in our case, the concept of chair is a simple representation made up in an arbitrary fashion. The material *truth* of the chair is the conceptual result of a datum considered crystallized, immobile, compact; but the nuclear physicist's concept of matter is different; for him, nothing is compact and definite, everything *becomes* and what becomes cannot be conceptualized and fixed. How can we stop the process of becoming? You have one perceptive conception of matter and the physicist has another, because you are both in a limited cognitive segment of the circumference. Knowledge, on the contrary, must spring from a Centre, from a *Point* which is neither of the personal, individual order, nor of the universal (as opposed to the particular) order. Only in this non-partial but *total* sphere of existence can we comprehend Totality.

From the metaphysical point of view, the piece of stone that the scientist investigates is nothing but a *flash*, because he barely manages to define it before it vanishes from his hands. Material forms fade into the non-formal. His own physical body which he perceives and is utilizing, is, in turn, a flash in the continuous flow of time or becoming. In any case, I would like you to consider that this flash is not an illusion; no phenomenon is an illusion in the Western sense of the term. Becoming, too, is such if compared to a *centre*, which does not become, which is outside of time. Our consciousness, alas, fluctuates according to the strength of becoming; it flows with time and continuously identifies with it; consequently, it undergoes the process without comprehending it. But perception is that which falsifies Reality. It gives us a sense of time, space, and causality, of movement and of process; it is, however, necessary to thoroughly examine whether this perception is capable of proper relationships and proper knowledge. We must make ourselves autonomous, detached agents and realize metaphysical Stillness, from which, being no longer overcome or impaired in any way by nature, we can comprehend its eternal changes.

Q. But isn't all we are saying pure nihilism?

R. If we did not give it a positive value or failed to recognize the Absolute as such, you would be right. The Absolute is, on the contrary, the only real Essence, the only Truth worthy of the name, and this Absolute is ourselves. This is the opposite of nihilism. The fact that the relative or phenomenal disappears is not a philosophical conjecture of ours: it is a statement of fact, which is self-evident. Science tells us that our planet is only a few billion years old. Let us recall once more that we are discussing the question from a realizative and metaphysical, not an empirical, religious, or occult point of view.

Q. I think that living a beautiful dream is always very pleasant. Why should I deprive myself of it?

R. Where there is beauty there is also ugliness, where there is pleasure there is also pain, where there is light there is also darkness. The individual seeks greedily to grasp and hold the former and to discard the latter, but that is impossible. Duality is a double-sided coin that cannot be split.

EVOLUTIONISM

Q. If I consider what we have said, I must discard the concept of evolution. Now, evolution is the cornerstone of many sciences, even of a number of spiritual ones. What can you say in this regard?

R. What do you mean by evolution? This is the point.[1]

– That manifestation goes from one stage to a more highly developed one, until it reaches final perfection.

R. If I am not mistaken, you want to state that something 'not perfect' can become 'perfect', that a 'minus' can become a 'plus', that a 'non-God' can become a 'God'. From a metaphysical point of view this is not possible. A flower is such because it is *already* such in the seed; otherwise it could not manifest itself as a flower. The whole of manifestation is a book that comes apart, states the Poet.[2]
In addition, the concept of becoming presupposes time and this is simply a mental product: it does not have an ontological reality. In the mind of God all is whole and present; but our consciousness, clouded by *māyā*, is unable

---
[1] See the chapter 'Evolutionism' in Raphael, *Tat tvam asi*, That thou art. Op. cit.

[1] Dante: as symbol of the initiate poet.

to embrace the Whole. The true Awakened man sees the end right from the very beginning.

– Did I not develop from birth? And am I not still evolving? Mentally I find it impossible to grasp the concept of non-evolution.

R. Not really evolving, but *revealing* what was enclosed in your embryo. Humanity is simply revealing what potentially it always had in the depth of its heart.

– So, what must I do in order to evolve, I mean, to realize myself?

R. To evolve, nothing. To realize yourself you must comprehend yourself and awaken to what you have always been and always will be.

Q. Can I realize myself in this life or must I be reincarnated many times?

R. If we are already the unconditioned Self, in any moment or place we can recover our nature of Being.

Q. How is it that so many die without achieving Realization?

R. What is it which dies and is born?
Subconscious egoic contents are so many and so strong that they present a serious obstacle to achieving consciousness of the Self. Realization is close or far away depending on the obstacles that come in between.

Q. There are many spiritual theories that teach us that only in a very distant cycle can one achieve final perfection. What do you think of this conclusion?

R. Realization does not depend on conditions of time; the latter, we have already seen, is a mental construction. Perfection exists already; it has always existed; it is in us, with us, and among us. In It we move, live and are.

Q. Can we grasp the Absolute and thereby achieve the highest level of initiation, while we are still on this planet? I have been told that Perfection can be achieved on other planets.

R. The Absolute exists on earth, in heaven and in every place. Were our planet not supported by the Absolute, it would become an absolute by itself, in opposition to the sole Absolute, the Real. Two absolutes cannot coexist. You yourself could not live if you did not contain this absoluteness; an empirical relative exists only insofar as it is sustained by the Absolute. On the other hand, it is obvious that if Realization does not depend on time it does not depend on space either. Space and time are mental constructions, logical forms and images useful to the mind that does not comprehend the Infinite and the eternal Present.

Q. There are, however, planets more evolved than ours where one can have suitable experiences.

R. But why this insistence on planetary and cosmic distinctions? Our solar system is simply one of the *neighbourhoods* of the galaxy. Travelling from one neighbourhood to another is nothing extraordinary. Life is One, distinctions and differences belong only to the separating and distinguishing mind which always needs to divide, to compartmentalize, to take apart in order to understand a simple grain of truth; but synthesis and unity escape it. Mind is time, space, and causality.

THE TEACHER

Q. What can I do to find a Teacher or *Guru*? I see that many are waiting for this encounter, and so I think it is necessary. Can you show me a way, or do you yourself want to be my *Guru*?

R. The aim of life is not to seek a Teacher, but Truth. When you love truth more than your ego, then the *Guru* will come to meet you; it could even be a book, a friend or better still your own Self, the Teacher in your heart.

— But there is a hierarchy of Teachers to be sought and served.

R. You must serve only Truth and this does not just dwell in Teachers, but in the hearts of all beings. When we serve Teachers we engage in the mutual combat because our Teacher is always better than the Teacher of others: the Teacher Jesus is better than the Teacher Gautama and vice versa; the Teacher Ramakrishna is better than St Francis and vice versa; the Saints of one's own religion are always better than those of another religion, and so on. The chain of *Gurus* of a certain type of *Yoga* is better than another chain of *Gurus* of other types of *Yoga*.

Love for a Teacher is not our goal, but love for Truth, which alone gives Liberation and Realization.

— Must we reject the Teachers?

R. I did not say to 'reject'. We are all somebody's teacher. Truth includes the Teachers and the whole of Life, and so by loving Truth you also love all past, present and future *Gurus*, whatever their race, religion and brotherhood.

— Why does every one look for a Teacher?

R. Because it is easier to seek a Teacher than Truth, easier to serve a Teacher than Truth, more comfortable to surrender to another individual than to Truth, and easier to serve passively than to seek in a creative way with a positive attitude.

— I have always thought that without Teachers humanity could not wake up.

R. As long as that central Sun shines in the heart of the system, It will illuminate the just and the unjust, the great and the small, the weak and the strong, criminals and Saints, regardless of men's opinions.

— Should I not invoke the Teacher Jesus? I am a Christian and I am therefore devoted to Jesus.

R. Why don't you evoke Love, seek Love, serve Love? Start serving Love and you will enter into the heart not of a single Teacher, but of Divinity itself, the Teacher of all Teachers. When you penetrate the One *Essence*, you will communicate with all the beings and things of the universe.

The Teacher

– Does the death of Jesus mean nothing to you?

R. That of Jesus, no; that of Love, yes. Jesus came back to life after only three days, fit and healthier than before, but I have yet to see Love sprout in the hearts of men. That day long ago, they did not offend and trample on Jesus, but on Love, Comprehension, Charity and Compassion.

Q. When I find myself in mental silence, what can I do to go deeper and deeper into the mystery of my existence?

R. When you are in that state, how can you ever determine thought and movement? It would mean falling back into the mental process or becoming. On the other hand, it is opportune to remember that the mere silence of the mind is just a window open on the Self, not actual Realization of the Self. When this silence is established for a long time in us as the natural consequence of detachment and of the elimination of all kinds of superimposition, then, sooner or later, we shall achieve awareness of the Self.

THE AWAKENED MAN

Q. How could the Self see the world of names and forms?

R. That 'could see' means that you are not yet the Self. And if you are not Self, why do you worry about something that is still remote?

– It could stimulate the awareness of the Self.

Q. The Awakened man sees only the Substratum of the whole, the unmoving screen without time, space, and causality, whereas the unawakened sees the evanescent and changing objects.

– Can you tell me how the Awakened man considers death? An unconscious fear of death dwells in me; I am obsessed with death.

R. For the Awakened man there is neither death nor birth, neither suffering nor sensory happiness. Fear – fear of all kinds – arises when the consciousness identifies with the conflicting ego.

– Why do you speak then of conflict and suffering?

R. I use a kind of language suited to the experience of the unawakened, who says he suffers or rejoices and so on, depending on circumstances.

– How can one recognize an Awakened man?

R. How can one recognize a scientist? What is the difference between a scientist and, let us say, an ordinary person? None on the outside; the difference is inside, in their mind and consciousness.

– Do you think you are an Awakened man?

R. The ego believes to be this or that; when it disappears, so does the entire question of distinction and qualification.

– Can you tell me how the problem of good and evil is seen by the Awakened man?

R. Some truths are better kept in the heart. The unawakened, living in duality and under the dominion of that samsāric ghost, which is the ego, might be astonished by or not understand certain things. If we are humble enough and courageous, Truth will make its way by stages in all of us. In any case, the problem of duality concerns the ego and not the Self.

Q. I don't know if this might just be simple curiosity on my part, but how does a living Liberated person move?

R. A *jīvanmukta* does not move, he does not produce imprisoning actions, nor does he create any kind of translational motion. He rotates on himself unveiling himself as Principle, without name or form. For the unawakened, the Awakened may be considered a mere abstraction.

Q. What mission might the Awakened man carry out?

R. There are many missionaries: scientists, artists, writers, saints, etc.; they all contribute to stimulate the hearts of human beings. Why limit the field to Saints, those who are Awakened, or to those who profess themselves to be spiritualists? To reach certain aims, the great Unity of Life makes use of a humble mother as well as a political or a scientific genius.

– There are, however, some particular missions of great scope.

R. These distinctions belong to the selective, comparing and competitive mind, not to the One-without-a-second.

ADVAITA

R. *Advaita* is quite a special way, let us say, a path that goes against the current. By understanding what is not reality it arrives at the acceptance of that which is Absolute. By rejecting the duality of subject and object , which is the basis of the thinking process, it arrives at the transcendence of thought, the mind itself, and the entire speculative sphere, including metaphysics. This road leads to authentic fullness, to Joy and Bliss without objects, to *sat-cit-ānanda* (pure Existence, pure Intelligence, and pure Bliss).[1]

The world of names and forms is a product of the cosmic Mind, and *avidyā* emerges when we consider this world as separate from the cosmic dreamer, a Reality in itself, an absolute. With the sword of discernment the *jñāni* separates phenomenon from noumenon, product from producer, and becoming from Being.

The process is one of back-tracking, because it is necessary to withdraw into the Centre of Being, gradually, without effort, without offering any resistance, without forcing the psyche or provoking any wilful action, but simply by making use of observation, of intuitive discernment and of meditation without an object.

---

[1] For further inquiry into this 'Way' of realization, see Raphael, The *Pathway of Non-Duality* (*Advaitavāda*), and specifically the '*Advaita Vedānta*' chapter. Aurea Vidyā, New York.

All human desire tends toward happiness, but this 'urge to research' that which produces Fullness is mistakenly directed outward, towards that which sensory perception calls change: hence conflict and consequent suffering. That which is changeable can never lead to anything stable, lasting, or constant.

Desire is simply the reflection of a forgotten joy, of a lost paradise. When we learn how to direct our energies towards the unchanging Centre of Being, then we shall find what we have lost.

When we recognize the fact that the outward-looking mind can produce only separation and conflict, we shall bring it back to a state of stillness or of silence rich with Life.

Q. Does this philosophical view not tie in with the absolute idealism of many Western philosophers?

R. Behind thought lies the mind, behind the mind lies the thinker, and behind thinking lies the Uncaused and Undetermined *Brahman*, the substratum of all. As you can see, it is not a matter of absolute idealism, since ultimate Reality does not coincide with the thinking state or with mind itself.

– But the manifest world becomes subjective.

R. Subject and object are nothing but mental modifications and prefabricated conceptualizations caused by a scission of the being. When you dream, you are in a subjective condition, and yet in your dream you perceive objects which apparently are so fully outside the subjective mental framework that the subject is influenced by them. But the subjective and the objective aspects of dreams are nothing but thought products: they are mind itself.

Remember that wherever an object exists there must also be a subject. These two are born simultaneously.

– Does the intelligible world exist thanks to my particular perception or subjective ideation?

R. Not exactly; this concept belongs to solipsism (subjective idealism). We can eliminate our own specific capacity to formulate ideas, but not *Brahmā*'s or *Īśvara*'s. Our dream, for greater clarity, takes place in a vaster ideation or dream. Thus, for us, the world that surrounds us is real; we call it objective until we enter into *Brahmā*'s consciousness. What took place before at the individual level of ideation, now occurs at the cosmic level. As you can see, the empirical world is at the same time real and unreal, subjective and objective; it depends on the state of consciousness and the particular existential level in which we want to position ourselves.

If we succeed in grasping all this, we shall have set in proper perspective the question that makes of 'perception' a cognitive possibility, and, even more importantly, the other question that sees the external object as independent of the perceiving subject.

– But where does the Awakened man fit into the framework of the ever-changing life?

R. It all depends on the level of awakening reached. Dualists stop at the Union with *Brahmā*, that is, with the manifest God, with the cosmic *Jīva*. *Advaita Vedānta*, through Realization of the One-without-a-second, soars beyond all possible dualities, and even transcends Unity itself, which is the cause of every manifestation.

— I begin to see that *Vedānta* is not that theory of illusion I had been told.

R. There is great misunderstanding on this point. The *Vedānta darśana* is realizative metaphysics (a merely speculative metaphysics always remains within the ambit of theoretical and discursive philosophy), and *advaita* metaphysics in particular represents the highest kind of realization known. Let us say that its vision is unique. Furthermore in the East the meaning attributed to the word 'illusion' is different from ours, and this must be kept in mind.

We have seen that, strictly speaking, dreams at night should not be considered illusion. Our various impressions, reactions, decisions are not illusory. On the one hand, when an event or datum succeeds in modifying our previous state of consciousness, it cannot be said to be an illusion. Illusion as such produces nothing. That snake we spoke of earlier, which modifies our consciousness, must have a point of departure or a real base on which to subsist. It cannot be born of nothing. In fact, its base is the rope. Illusion and error consist in mistaking something for something else: that is, after all, the condition of *māyā*. *Māyā* causes a thing to appear different from what it really is.[1] There are two sides to *māyā*: one is *projection* (the image of the snake); the other one is *veiling* (because the projected image in turn covers the real object, the rope). Therefore *māyā* is not illusion in the Western sense of the word.

— Is this why intuitive discrimination is so highly regarded?

R. We stated elsewhere that man bases himself not on reality as such (the rope) but on the image of that reality

---

[1] See also, *Dṛigdṛsyaviveka*, attributed to Śaṅkara. Op. cit.; also the chapter 'The mystery of *māyā* or appearance' in Śaṅkara, *Vivekacūḍāmaṇi*. Op. cit.

(the snake) which his mind projects. Here lies his necessity to continually adjust his *interpretation* of the world. This is clearly seen in his conceptions of God and matter. These concepts, down the ages, have undergone numerous interpretations or conceptual modifications.

– Is there a real base to *māyā*?

R. If it were real we could not eliminate it. Let me give you an example: when instead of the snake we recognize the rope as the ultimate reality, what happens to *māyā*? Try to intuit this mystery.

I want to underline that we are speaking of facts, occurrences, events that are in front of us; we could abandon *Vedānta* terminology and even its vision, but the problem would remain with us just the same. These mistaken perceptions and interpretations of data dwell within us, they constitute a fact, and therefore we must do something. We are not laying down dogmas, strict philosophical schemes or convictions to be accepted or rejected *en bloc*. Nor is it a question of propaganda in favour of one system or another. We are simply investigating a certain kind of human experience, a mode of thinking, a type of psychological behaviour which unfortunately causes error and conflict.

SUBJECT AND OBJECT

Q. I would like to go back to the concept of subject and object.[1] It is important, at least for me. You said that it is an ideation of ours. In what sense? What can these two terms correspond to?

R. Can we look into this question together? Let us begin with ideation at night. Is there a dreaming subject?

Q. Yes, I am the one dreaming.

R. Are you sure?

– I think that I have no doubt about it. Somebody else cannot dream for me.

R. Thus the mind is the subject that projects images, entire universes, isn't that true?

– Did we not say some days ago that the mind is only a vehicle?

---

[1] For further reference, see also Raphael, *The Pathway of Non-Duality*. Op. cit.

R. Yes, but also that it possesses certain characteristics, certain ways of operating and peculiar qualities of its own. Just as the glands produce certain secretions, so the mind secretes innumerable projections or thought images. On the other hand, is it not the mind that dreams?

– Without a doubt, the mystery of being lies in the mind or in what we call the mind.

R. Quite, that is not so wrong. In any case, the mind secretes thoughts that take on the characteristics of mental waves or modifications. A mental modification is represented by the image or concept: perceiving subject. Where there is a perceiving subject, there must also be an object; thus the mind itself, with its ideation or its projection of indefinite data, produces the object as well. Subject and object are mental productions.

– What? Isn't the subject the ego? Isn't it myself?

R. Let us see. When you wake up you recognize that, after all, your experience during the night was nothing but a dream. In other words, the *waking subject* no longer accepts the previous experience of the *dreaming subject*. In fact, in waking up you discover yourself, let's say, as a different person. On the other hand, if the object of the dream disappears, then the corresponding subject must vanish too. If the subject were always the same nocturnal one, on awakening one should still be the subject of that particular world, but, instead, we have to choose to be either one or the other.

– Is this subject, then, the actor who plays various roles in the drama of life?

R. We can say that. And depending on how our various roles remain chiselled out in our psychical substance (mind and emotions) they may from time to time re-emerge; and, if we are not in accord or in harmony with the ego or subject of that particular moment, they may even provoke conflicts and complexes.

— I have a better understanding of the importance of restraining thought. This subject is, therefore, the one that experiences certain things, that rejoices or worries. But where is the ego, my being, that is, my living reality, where does it live, and what does it do? If that subject is a product of the mind, there must be another entity which supports everything, I think.

R. My brother, this evening we are entering into the heart of a very important question. We must understand each other. We must discover who we are and who we are not. We must discriminate between what is mere contingency in us and what is eternal Beatitude, and recognize what is ego and what is not ego. Thus we shall be able to discard what we are not and consider ourselves for what we are. But before continuing, I would like to say that we are speaking of *realizative metaphysics*, which can be effected insofar as we transform our mental vision. *Comprehension* occurs when we *live* a particular state of consciousness. Erudition leads to nothing. If, for example, we test the recognition which we have shared this evening, we shall pay attention to mental productions so that they do not occur either at night, in dreams, or during the day. When we approach a beautiful flower, we immediately have the perceiving subject and the object. This, in turn, causes pleasure, and the perceiving subject rejoices. If after a while we change the scene and are no longer in front of a lovely flower but a repugnant object, we have another subject and an object which arouses anguish, anxiety, and repulsion. The present subject is not the same as the former one; if it were we would have an absolute value, which in this case should be an ever joyful subject. On the contrary, it is not absolute, and so we have a different subject and object every instant; as a result, our reaction is always different, fluctuating, and changing.

– I agree with this clarification of yours. Mere curiosity does not reveal reality; I have taken notes already so that I can re-examine and come to a better understanding of what we have discovered together. I have reached the point of understanding that experience is undertaken by this subject that is produced by the mind. But there are other things I need to understand.

– (Another speaker). This reminds me of the upaniṣadic parable of the two birds that dwell in the same tree; one produces action and experience, while the other remains immobile, silent and impassive.

R. We can take up this image because it helps us to understand so many things. One moment! Have you finished with your question? (Turning to the speaker before last).

– I would like to find out who lies behind this entire process.

R. First of all, have you understood that all that springs from the mind is changing, orbital movement, continuous modification? Have you understood that this movement is relative, phenomenal, and that until today you have attributed, up to now, absolute value to it? Our intention, by contrast, is to look within ourselves for the Absolute, the eternally valid, the constant, that which does not depend on fluctuations or reactions produced by a capricious subject and object. If what we have examined is incompleteness, where can we look for Joy without an object? The mind is nothing but conflict and duality; it produces the experiencing subject and the object of experience; the object may be offered by our subconscious, where the various impressions are recorded, or by the world around us, but whether it is inside or outside us matters little.

We have seen the image of the two birds: the first represents the unstable, mobile experiencer and karmic enjoyer; he rejoices, is satisfied, or suffers; in other words he experiences duality. The second corresponds to the Witness who does not participate in the enslaving games of the experiencer. The first is the planet earth with its orbital movement; the second is the sun, always identical to itself and rotating on its own axis, the silent witness of all earthly events.

Once this entire process has been understood, the next step is no longer to share in mental action and gradually, but persistently, to create a condition of quiet, calm, and absence of thought and of subject and object. When we are masters of our own thinking process, we shall turn our eyes towards the Witness, who can be comprehended only in total mental silence. The mind would otherwise just create new projections and then speculate on these mental representations; in other words, we would fall into the same mistake into which we have fallen until now.

Every vehicle of the *jiva* experiencer expresses itself in a certain way, possesses certain qualities, and presents certain characteristics. When the jiva passively follows the expressions of the vehicles, then we identify with those vehicles. We perceive ourselves to be one with those vehicles, instead of remembering that we are entities distinct from them. When this happens we say: I am this, or I am that; I am weak, or I am strong; I am anguished, or I am happy; I am young, or I am old; I am rich, or I am poor; I am learned, or I am ignorant; I am a slave, or I am free.[1]

Q. I wonder if the vehicles have not been created by the mind itself.

R. If we examine the question from the scientific view that matter is nothing but electricity at various degrees of condensation, we must conclude that the mind can solidify its images, can render them, let us say, materialized. The vehicles are electricity at various degrees of condensation. What the mind has produced the mind can dissolve and transcend.

— If I manage to extrapolate a thought from all the vehicles and objects, making it pure and uncontaminated, can I comprehend Totality?

R. Whoever takes himself to the *cit* principle (pure intelligence and consciousness) is already in *Brahman*. This is *sat-cit-ānanda*, and we can attain it also through any one of these three principial modes.

Q. I realize that with ever greater understanding of the mind, its mechanisms and its behaviour, I can transcend all the other types of *Yoga* that I have followed. At present I am following *Bhakti Yoga*, but I think that comprehension of thought is very important. What do you advise?

---

[1] See also, *Dṛgdṛṛsyaviveka*, attributed to Śaṅkara. Op. cit.

R. I cannot point you to a path, nor encourage you to leave a certain kind of teaching. You must discover the right answer for yourself. In general, we can say that only by questioning our own thought process can we know it and resolve it. When we comprehend thought and its dynamics, we shall already be beyond the mind and its selective, empirical thought.

TIME

– At times I think that perhaps I am not destined to achieve realization during this cycle of my existence. How can I free myself of this thought?

R. What is time? What are past, present, and future? What is meant by low, medium, and high?

To define these data we need an initial term of comparison, an 'immobile' point of reference. Now, where does the future lie? What basis or 'immobile' point can we make it spring from?

– From the present.

R. Which present?

– The state of consciousness in which I find myself at the moment.

R. The moment we are speaking of is already... past.

– Well then, the past is that 'immobile' from which the future is born.

R. So we have it that the future is a time yet to come, while the past has already gone; now, will the *occurred* ever be able to produce the not-occurred? Will the already born ever be able to produce the non-born? Will fact ever be able to produce a non-fact? On the other hand, in order to consider it past, we must compare it to something else which permits us to presume a 'before' related to an 'afterward'.

— We said that the future is born of the past, and so this future is our term of reference.

R. But the future is the not-occurred, the non-existent, a pure abstraction, a simple mental representation.

— Then the present is that 'immobile' from which certainty is born because I am aware I am living it.

R. If you are conscious of living the present, that means that your *attention*, and therefore your awareness, is always in a state of Identity with your 'Presence' and this Identity constitutes the immediate reality. But to experience this state of suspension of thought is difficult.

Q. I have experienced the state you have just described and I must admit that in such a state one cannot entertain the notion of past and future.

R. Note that the gentleman speaks of the *notion* of past and future. I believe we are beginning to understand something.
So when we live Identity we can experience nothing except our true Essence, always identical to itself. On the other hand, when we fall into ideation the various notions of time emerge; the past emerges from *recollection*. If we had no recollection we would have no past, but recollection

is memory of 'something'. Time exists insofar as we relate it to *things*, to objects, events. Our yesterday is simply a certain event, a process in which recollection brings us back, not to 'yester-time', which does not exist, but always to today. We can say it brings us back to the present but projects a content which repeats and perpetuates itself, thereby imprisoning us in crystallization and the process of becoming. It follows that time is a 'sensory object'. Now, all sensory objects are nothing but ideations and mental representations which live on relativity. To escape from representation or ideation means to be released from the time-event framework as well. To live the present means realizing identity with the Self which does not depend on any mental image, and hence not on time either. To conclude: being a mere datum of perception, time cannot be real or absolute. Beyond time stands the solitary Witness as the substratum of the entire process of perception.

The mind creates hours, minutes, seconds; it creates years and aeons, but all these are simply the mind's fleeting conceptualizations and crystallizations to make us feel calm and reassured. It produces 'images' to obtain security and perpetuity, but also conflict and misery. Not grasping timelessness, which is Absoluteness, the mind moulds formal constructions to compensate for its incompleteness.

Is it not the mind that seeks to conceptualize the nameless, the spaceless, and the causeless or what it considers as the Unknown? Its ideations are always based on the known, because mind itself is time, becoming and sensory experience. Did the mind not construct the idea of God, nature, the individual, etc., according to its own way of projecting and imagining? What the mind calls divinity is always an idea fitted to its limited time-space, always an object of perception, and therefore a product, a process, and an accumulation.

IMMORTALITY AND BLISS

Q. I am deeply religious and I want to ask you if on my death I can reach immortality, having of course followed all the precepts required of me at present.

R. Who is it in you that poses this question?

– What do you mean! I am the one who is asking.

R. Allow me to explain: is it the Absolute in you, the uncaused Spirit or is it your ego, your individualized and solidified mind?

– (After some hesitation) The ego is asking... I think, the individualized mind.

R. This ego-ghost, knowing that it must die, seeks immortality, perpetuity and becoming. But will what is mortal ever become immortal? Will what is fleeting and passing ever perpetuate itself? Can what belongs to time ever belong to the timeless?

– What should I ask of God? How should I pray?

R. Ask yourself again: who is it in me that *wants* something?

– If we must not ask or pray to God, who is our Father, what do religious teachings exist for? Religions do not exist only in the West.

R. When the ego is weak, thirsty and hungry, it prays to God and obeys religious commandments, even the hardest to follow. When, on the other hand, the ego is proud, full of itself, no longer hungry, then it turns its back on religion and on the temple. The ego is a monster of desires which, when satisfied, immediately turns its gaze elsewhere in search of further prey.

– Why should I not seek my soul's Bliss?

R. Either the soul possesses Bliss in itself or it will never be able to acquire it. We cannot obtain what we do not potentially possess.

– What should I do then to find Bliss and the grace of God?

R. You have only to comprehend Bliss, comprehend what are the obstacles that prevent its realization, and meditate on what *one is*. Thus, you must not await bodily death in order to reveal Bliss and immortality because you can reveal them during life, with your eyes wide open, your mind silent, tranquil and at peace.

Q. You speak of *ānanda* or Bliss without an object. What does this mean? Can you explain it more clearly?

R. *Ānanda* is spontaneous, natural, innocent, and unsought Joy or Bliss; in it there is no desiring ego that takes possession of something, that exalts itself. In sensory happiness there is pleasure, a search for enjoyment, a plan, and expectations, emotional heightening, and memory.

In *ānanda* there is no duality, no emotional conflict; there is no memory, and no acquisition. *Ānanda* is not the gratification of any sensory urge, and so it is not relief of tension.

In pleasure the ego exalts itself; in *ānanda* the ego is annulled.

Ānanda may stem from the simple contemplation of a clod of earth, the sound of falling water, or a field full of poppies, a human face, or a silvery reflection of the moon; if during this contemplation a quest for something, a desire, or an urge for possession enters into play, then the ānanda enchantment vanishes and pleasure emerges. This is self-gratification, the result of dissatisfaction, of frustration: the individual is in a state of conflict and tries to solve it by looking for pleasure; thus pleasure is but a fleeting illusion to soothe dissatisfaction.

Love is *ānanda* because in love there is no ego, no expectation, no request, no gratification.

Q. Why does the urge to be superior to others exist in so many?

R. The ego knows it is impotent, miserable and contingent, and so it invents all possible ways to compensate for this lack of completeness; but its superiority is precarious, fleeting, and illusory. No sense of superiority can offer completeness, at most a sensory thrill or pleasure which is dual, and therefore conflictual. There are many 'egos' which, although aware of the fact that others approach them and submit to them because of some specific temporal position they occupy, do not care about these others.

In order that it may go on living, the ego continuously begs for compensation; to pick up some homage and recognition, it forgoes all dignity. The ego sells itself, even for very little, in order to appear what it is not.

THERE ARE VARIOUS PATHWAYS

Q. At present I am practising *Haṭha Yoga*, and these exercises or *āsanas* are very beneficial: I feel more alert, more vigorous than ever before, more competent in my job. For me this is completeness and fullness. Why don't you advise people to do this kind of *Yoga*?

R. There are those who seek fullness of the body, others fullness of the mind, and others fullness of pure Spirit. It depends on their inner needs.
– Can a healthy and vigorous body not lead in turn to completeness of the soul?

R. If this were true, the whole of humanity would be perfectly accomplished and live in integral fullness; in fact, the sick are very few compared to the many that are healthy and vigorous, especially in the West.

Q. In these conversations we have spoken of *Bhakti Yoga*, *Haṭha Yoga* and *Yogadarśana*; I seem to understand that there are several paths. Could you give some indications?

R. The traditional East has met with the needs of people in an intelligent and non-dogmatic way in their approach to Reality or Divinity. To this end it has pointed out different ways. According to the traditional Eastern teachings, the human being is characterized by three guṇas or qualities: *sattva* (harmony), *rajas* (activity) and *tamas* (inertia), and these *guṇas* determine the psycho-energetic differences among individuals.

The tamasic individual is conditioned by material, physical and pranic qualifications, and is slow, sluggish and instinctive. The rajasic person is extroverted, passionate, and he acts before thinking; brilliant and restless, he easily shows his inner side. The sattvic being is harmonious, contemplative, and tends towards reflection and abstraction.

– Can the three *guṇas* be found in the same individual?

R. Yes, certainly, even though one *guṇa* may be predominant.

Q. You have mentioned the individual differences at the psycho-energetic level; how do the different types of *Yoga* meet these differences?

R. The different paths respond to the qualifications of whoever is undertaking the way; and according to the level of awakening of one's consciousness they relate to the individual's three bodies of manifestation: physical, emotional, and mental.

Considering certain types of *Yoga*, we can very briefly say that *Haṭha Yoga* takes as its support the physical body and the vital functions, *Bhakti Yoga* focuses its attention on the emotional body, and *Rāja Yoga* deals with the mind.[1]

---

[1] For further reference see also Raphael, *Essence and Purpose of Yoga*, The Initiatory Pathway to the Transcendent. Aurea Vidyā, New York.

OCCULTISM AND PSYCHIC POWERS

Q. I study occultism; I have followed, more or less, all of these conversations. I am somewhat perplexed. I have a question: Can you tell me how can I make use of the occult in order to achieve realization?

R. This you must find out for yourself. What is occultism, or what do you mean by this name?

— Occultism addresses and studies all supernatural phenomena. It seeks to understand the invisible or suprasensory world. Objective facts have their causes in the subjective world: all this is very interesting; it makes so many things clear to me.

R. Do you think that knowledge of the many natural phenomena can help you free yourself from conflict? The real occultists are those scientists who, day after day, discover the causal combinations behind many effects. Don't you think that these atomic scientists, those who discover the atom's energy, are true magicians? But can knowledge of vital phenomena, however worthy of attention and investigation, really resolve the causes of human conflict? Can it sweep away the ego's envy, pride, vanity, competitiveness and misery?

Do you think that the acquisition of a power, be it human or superhuman, can solve man's fundamental problems?[1]

– The ego completes itself through expansion. Every acquisition of knowledge integrates the individual. I fail to understand why the power of knowledge must be excluded or considered immoral when for the human individuality, self-assertion – for example – is its best completion. If we look around us we see that most suffering is due to the ego's inability to gratify its needs and desires and to react to certain facts. If nature has those powers to offer, why not allow a person to use them to master things, and even life itself?

R. If I am not mistaken, we might sum up this question as follows: the ego is impotent, weak and powerless in the face of certain phenomena/events; if we give it the appropriate instruments of power it will grow strong, capable, masterful, and therefore we will achieve happiness, bliss and fulfilment. So we can conclude that if someone is sick we should give him the possibility of being healed, and he will attain bliss; if he is poor, let us give him wealth, and he will be joyful; if someone is unable to fly, let us give him the means to do so and he will be blissful; if he wants to kill, let us allow him to do so and he will be happy; and if he is an obscure but ambitious character, let us give him a position of great social prestige and he will be satisfied.

According to the gentleman who asked the question, conflict, suffering, and effort – that is, illness, poverty, hunger, ambition, envy, and so on – can be solved by offering the ego the chance to gratify its desires. But in order

---

[1] See also the chapter 'The Siddhis' in Raphael, *The Pathway of Non-Duality*. Op. cit.

to satisfy any desire whatsoever one needs the appropriate power/instrument.

What is a power? Can you help me to define it?

— For me, a power is the ability through which one can influence someone or something.

R. But in order to exercise power, at whatever level, there must be, on the one hand, the holder of power, and on the other, the object/event which submits to power; besides, of course, power itself.

To wield power, therefore, three data are necessary: the holder of power, the power-instrument or medium of power, and the object on which to exercise it. I would like to underline the fact that *power* in itself and for itself is impersonal and depends on the direction one wants to give to it. Thus the energy or power of the atom is impersonal; depending on its use, the outcome is either beneficial or harmful.

Going back to our threefold division, it can be deduced that power does not represent the subject or the holder of power. Thus to identify the holder of power with power itself means falling into ignorance or *avidyā*; it means mistaking the rope for the snake. Many occultists fall into this error, that is why they are called 'worshippers of *Hiraṇyagarbha*' (the world of energy or power).

What matters is to understand the *holder* of power rather than power itself, which is a merely qualitative attribute. We must understand what we really are, we must arrive at the ultimate Essence, at the Absolute within us which does not depend on qualities or attributes of any kind whatsoever.

Q. Can power solve man's misery and conflict?

R. We are going around in circles. Does material wealth, which is one kind of power, solve man's true, innermost problem? The West is rich, but has it solved its conflictual problem? Can any sort of *fame* (of the ego), which is another kind of power, eliminate suffering? Has the dictator who holds the power for an entire nation in his hands achieved bliss? Man possesses the greatest power conceivable nowadays: nuclear energy; can we say that through it humanity has achieved bliss?

There is yet another fundamental point: all power, whether human or superhuman, requires an urge to be satisfied and matured. A power without the urge to exercise it ceases to be such and no longer exists.

Power is the 'capacity to influence', but even if the slightest desire to influence springs up in us, we find ourselves already in a state of conflict, and so we are not truly fulfilled. One who has reached Completeness does not need to influence others. One who has reached the Centre within himself has achieved *isolated Unity*, the Absolute, and in this Unity there cannot be a second on whom to wield any influence whatsoever.

Q. (The same questioner who asked about occultism earlier). If occultism is interested in power and energies, then I cannot find my ultimate Reality through it. What would you advise me to do?

R. I am not against any kind of speculation; there are teachings which concern only the form-aspect of life, others which deal with the quality or psychological aspects of life, and yet others which deal with that One or All, that is Life itself and which lies behind all this changing scenario. Whether we approach one or the other kind of knowledge depends on our inner response. Thus, presumably, whoever moves in the direction of the Absolute has ceased to fool with (or be fooled by) the *qualifying* and *qualified world.*

The initiatory maturity of the Being can be deduced from the direction taken by his consciousness.

Q. When you speak of the Life aspect, are you referring to the Vedantic *Brahman* or *ātman*?

R. Yes, but it is not life in the ordinary sense.

— Therefore, to achieve this Completeness you are talking about, is it not necessary to transcend the entire objective and subjective world?

R. Certainly; just as to transcend the objective world we must overcome resistance offered by *mass* and *force*, in the same way to transcend the subjective world we must overcome the resistance of the *energies* and *powers* which continuously compel us to enchaining action, enslaving extroversion, and conflict. We must remember that, despite all subjective and objective resistance, we are the Absolute, *ātman*, *Brahman*, the non-born, the uncaused and timeless. Our true Reality dwells beyond all subject and object or duality.

ART

Q. Let's say that I am a creative person, an artist; do you think that it is possible to reach the ultimate Reality through art?

R. What do we mean by creation? Nothing is created or destroyed, but everything is transformed. In fact, we simply *transform* ideas or intuitions into colours, words, music, etc., and these forms of music, colour, and so on change in time and space. Thus we have a nineteenth-century colour form which is no longer congenial to us and a thirteenth-century literary form which is no longer acceptable. We must not restrict the field of *ideal transformation* only to those we call artists. Thousands and thousands of human beings are artists, and more often than not are totally unknown. But the determining factor or the subject *operandi* (acting subject) is the ego which qualifies that transformation according to its contents, its limitations, its incompleteness and its sensitivity.

When the intuited archetypes flow unimpeded, not held back by colourings of the ego, then idea and expression are totally commensurate, and so are content and form, and the world of cause and effect.

Art and all other channels of creative expression are simply means and must not be confused with the ultimate Reality; but, as one gradually approaches the One-without-a-second, all instruments are transcended, because they no longer serve the purpose. Thus, in the ascent towards the One, every scripture be it sacred or profane, every *Yoga* technique, and every teaching, whether metaphysical or not, is lost and discarded as something which has served its end.

To find oneself the prisoner of an instrument or a channel of expression, or the prisoner of the manifest product itself, means to be crystallized at a specific point.

THE PATHWAY OF FIRE

CONTEMPLATION OF ACTION

1. When you experience an emotion (fear, anguish, pleasure, pain, etc.), become aware of the one who is experiencing the event. Ask yourself: *who* is enjoying the fruit of perception?

2. If you are observing something, like a tree, a table or a house, etc., ask yourself: who is observing?

3. If you are *thinking* of something, interrupt the flow of your thoughts and ask yourself: *who* is it who is thinking? What relationship is there between I who am thinking and the thought or image? Which of the two is the *constant*, the *invariant*?

4. If your gross physical body is hurt, ask yourself: who feels the pain? Do you consider yourself exclusively as a physical body? Then why are you suffering? Do you not see that this heap of flesh and bones is hardly born and is already rotting? Why do you abuse your nature, which is that of experiencing pleasure and pain? If you believe that you are the physical body, abandon yourself to its nature, which is your nature, and follow the rhythms of its being. But if you believe that *That* which experiences is beyond

the experienced and the experience itself, then what do you have to do with conflictive dualism, and the gross, physical body with its modifications? If *you are* immortal, then what do you have to do with that which *is not* immortal? Then tear this reflection of consciousness (which makes you feel what you are not) away from the perishable and fleeting world of *māyā*, rectify the belief that you are this or that and fly to embrace *That*.

5. Waking up one morning, you said to yourself: Today I shall carry out this intention, this project. By evening, though, you had to admit that your plan had not been executed. Why? If you are a single consciousness, a single will without a second, if you are a unique intelligence, it is absolutely impossible for your resolve to be frustrated or impeded by something or someone that does not exist. If your decision was diverted, it must mean that you are not alone, and not unity; it means that there is an opposing *second* within you; that there are two of you. And of these two, which one resolves, which one asserts itself? Who is it that *really* decides and proposes? If there are two of you, or three or four, there cannot be unity of intent. When many discordant voices devour your consciousness, you are in a state of deep conflict, you are torn apart by the monster with a thousand heads.

Have you thought of how to solve the problem of your duality, your conflicts, and your fragmentation? You can read the *Vedas*, the *Purāṇas*, and all the philosophies and learned essays ever written, but if you do not try to solve your constraining samsaric problem by yourself, there is no text that can offer you the solution and give you *Realization*.

6. If, on waking up one morning, you committed yourself to doing something that you ended up not doing, it means that you did not really wake up.

7. You are indulging too much in producing thoughts, in giving birth to ideas, in proposing images. Be careful! You are tying yourself up in a close web that sooner or later will imprison you, bind you, and abuse you.

'We become what we think. This is the eternal mystery', says the *Upaniṣad*.[1]

If you do not comprehend and direct your nature, it will annihilate you.

Onanists delight in manipulating thought. Those, on the other hand, who affirm are the ones who think and are.

The idea must become flesh or expression.

One who has decided cannot wait or allow thought to wander in that underworld of incompleteness which is without hope.

Whoever knows how to assert will possess immortality.

8. At night, covered with dust and exhaustion, dare to recognize all the alibis that your ego has created in order to escape the resolving axe.

The ego thirsts for supports. At night ask yourself: How many supports have I had to beg for?

9. In order to avoid its own death, the ego instinctively exploits your sentimentality and even some of your ideologies. The ego makes you believe that you must give yourself, that you belong to others, that you must work for the unfortunate, or that isolation is against altruism, and other things of this kind. I must tell you: Beware, the ego

---

[1] *Maitry Upaniṣad* VI.34.3.

is trapping you, and postponing its departure; the ego is caressing your ears with music that may sound sublime.

10. The ego resorts to pleasantness, vanity, velvet pride. One of the many pleasures is that of feeling useful, indispensable, essential. All egos feel they are missionaries of one kind or another: political, economic, cultural or spiritual. There is not a single ego that does not speak in the name of an ideal, an ethical code, or a philosophy; but strangely enough, these things are always for somebody else, never for us.

11. Let us be serious: whoever intends to dig his grave with his own hands has no time to believe he is either this or that, or to go here and there begging for useless and inappropriate supports, or to find compensatory alibis.

12. If you feel the impulse 'to act ', ask yourself the reason for this action.
If you feel an incentive to speak, ask yourself the reason for your words.

13. Whoever is busy throwing off the nightmares of an anguishing dream has no time to play around with beliefs, morals and social philosophies.

14. My friend, tell me: are you learned in the *Qabbālāh*, Sufism, and Pythagoreanism, or in Magic, the *Veda* and things of this kind?
Are you perhaps now trying to trap someone with your erudition?
Do you feel safe from loopholes and the unforeseen?
Are you, perhaps, looking for an opponent in order to knock him down with your sophisticated rhetoric?

Are you, perhaps, planning to play yet another role on the great stage of life?

My friend, listen to me: put all this verbal ability aside and nail your mind to silence, nail your vanity to the cross of *Realization*.

15. If you are really on the road to *vidyā*, write on the wall of your room: Here we are intent on dying, and not on offending.

16. Perhaps someone is urging you to live with others, at close contact with others, side by side with others, and trying to convince you that this means loving humanity. Friends' advice, as usual! Recognize the fact that one can live in a cave at the top of the Himalayas and still be deeply united with humanity, feeling for humanity and with humanity.

Whoever thinks that he can love man by touching his elbow or his hand is fooling himself. But self-delusion is also believing that one can offer to others the possibility of satisfying their desires.

17. Perhaps you have followed the extreme left, then the extreme right; then, in the end, disillusioned, you have opted for the centre, to be even more disappointed. I understand! You are confused.

Where can you turn? Are you, perhaps, binding yourself to isolation and scepticism? This, too, is a way, but not the right one.

Anyone who chooses the horizontal line will always meet the two extremes and the midpoint. This is the serpent that bites its own tail. Why not try to abandon the horizontal line and follow the vertical one?

The point at the centre is the apex of the triangle, and not the base where, in fact, you encounter the two extremes and the midpoint.

> 'That things have being, O Kaccāna, is one extreme;
> That things do not have being is the other extreme.
> These two extremes, O Kaccāna, have been avoided by Tathāgata,
> And this is the middle way that he teaches.'[1]

18. 'The middle way is without middle or sides; when your mind is perturbed you are on one side, and when it is not perturbed you are on the other side. When nothing of this exists, there is no middle way, and this is the middle way'.

19. If you live in simplicity there are no desires or cravings, and if there are no desires you are in peace, because you have transcended the cause of restlessness and conflict. Be simple, innocent, poor; reveal divine Indifference, and when you walk leave no footprints.

20. Struggling desperately to acquire something which vanishes like magic is madness. And yet how much energy, how much violence, is used to acquire things which, as soon as we have them in our hands, disappear!

O miserable thirst for illusions! O Enchantment of seducing mirages! You, who oblige millions of beings to live in fleetingness and oblivion; you, who deride the weak and the greedy, bow docilely to the one who dares to rend your deceitful veil.

---

[1] *Saṁyutta Nikāya* II.I.15.7.

21. 'Without leaving the house
one can know the world.
Without looking out of the window
one can learn the ways of Heaven.
The further afield one goes
the less one knows.
This is why the Wise Man,
although not walking, arrives,
although not looking, knows the names (of things),
although not acting, acts.'[1]

22. 'By studying you acquire something every day
with the Tao you lose something each day,
you lose more and more
until you come to non-action...'[2]

---

[1] Lao-Tze, *Tao Tè Ching* II.47.
[2] *Ibidem* II.48.

JĪVANMUKTA

23. Just as there are elementary particles that enter and leave earthly electromagnetic fields without undergoing any change whatsoever, so there are souls that enter and leave the electromagnetic field of the human race without undergoing any kind of attractive or repulsive modification.
These souls are called Liberated, Realized, *jīvanmukta*.

24. Every action or simple sensory movement, every modification of consciousness, is something incomplete.

25. 'I am identical to myself because I have no parts, I am beyond action and non-action. He who is One, infinite and eternal, and sky-like, how can he move?' (Śaṅkara, *Vivekacūḍāmaṇi*: 502).

26. "How could I have merit or demerit, I who am without organs, without mind, without modifications and without form...?' (*Ibid.*: 503).

27. 'The Witness is not touched by the properties of things because he is distinct from them, because he is without modifications and is indifferent, like a lamp which sheds light into a room without being affected by the properties of the room' (*Ibid.*: 505).

28. 'As the sun is witness to men's actions, as fire destroys everything without distinction, as the piece of rope is linked to what is superimposed on it, so I am identical to myself, impassible *ātman*, supreme intelligence' (*Ibid.*: 506).

29. 'I no longer act, nor do I make others act; I do not experience, nor do I make others experience, I do not see, nor do I make others see; I am the resplendent and transcendent *ātman*' (*Ibid.*: 507).

30. 'Whether this inanimate body falls here or there, on the earth or in the sea, is of no concern to me, because I am untouched by its properties, as air is untouched by a jar' (*Ibid.*: 509).

31. 'If ten, a hundred or a thousand different modifications take place in prakṛti, what part do I have in them, I who am absolute knowledge? Can the clouds ever scratch the sky?' (*Ibid.*: 511).

32. There are no modifications, changes, or perturbations of Reality: there are only various aspects of *māyā*.
Supreme Reality remains forever unchanged, unconditioned; it is *māyā*, phenomenon, which appears and disappears, which is and is not.

33. 'O blessed one, in this stinking body, this insubstantial heap of bones, skin, muscles, marrow, flesh, sperm, blood, mucus, tears, saliva, excrement, urine, air, bile and fat, of what use can enjoyment of desires be? In this body riddled with yearning, wrath, lust, illusion, fear, exhaustion, jealousy, separation from what is loved, union with what is abhorred, hunger, thirst, old age, death, illness, suffering, and so on, of what use can the satisfaction of desires be?

We see, moreover, that this entire universe is as perishable flies and other insects, or like the blades of grass and the trees of the forest that grow and decay? But why speak of these? There are others [beings], more powerful [than these]: they are great warriors, conductors of worlds (*cakravartin*) such as Sudyumna, Bhūridyumna, Indradyumna, Kuvalayāśva, Yauvanāśva, Vadhryaśva, Aśvapati, Śaśabindu, Hariścandra, Ambarıśa, Ananakta, Saryāti, Yayāti, Anaraṇya, Ukṣasena and many more; but kings, too, like Marutta or Bharata and other lesser men, who, after abandoning their vast prosperity before the very eyes of their families, departed from this world [to go] to that world. But why [trouble yourself] with them? In fact, there are others [still] higher [than they, but destined to come to an end: we can see the extinctions of the Gandharvas, the Asuras, the Yakśas, the Rākṣasas, the Bhūtas, the Gaṇas, the Piśācas, the god-snakes, vampires, and so on. But why [trouble yourself] with them? After all, with regard to other matters, there is the drying up of the great oceans, the collapse of mountain peaks, the displacement of the polestar, which is [considered to be eternally] fixed, the snapping of the ropes of the winds [which hold the heavenly bodies in their places], the sinking of the earth, and the withdrawal of the gods from their seats. In this cyclical process of becoming (*saṁsāra*), what use is the satisfaction of desires? One who feeds only on them is seen to return here [to this world] again and again. However, you must express yourself! In this cyclical process of becoming I am like a frog in a waterless well. O blessed one, you are our pathway [to liberation]; you are our pathway.'[1]

---

[1] *Maitry Upaniṣad* I. 3-4.

34. 'As to the person who is devoid of desire, has liberated himself from desire, and has attained the object of his desire because he desires nothing but the *ātman*, his vital breaths do not leave him; being just *Brahman*, he resolves himself into *Brahman*.

In this respect there is the following verse:

"When all desires which dwell in the heart have dissolved, then the mortal becomes immortal and even here enjoys *Brahman*"' (*Bṛhadāraṇyaka Up.*: IV, IV, 6-7).

35. 'In the sublime, golden sheath the *Brahman* abides, pure and undivided; this is the splendour, the light of lights: known by those who know the *ātman*.

In Him the sun shines not, the moon shines not, the stars shine not. There lightning does not flash, and certainly not this fire. All is splendour and all that exists shines of His light. This is the immortal *Brahman*; the *Brahman* which extends endlessly east, west, north, and south, above and below. *Brahman* is all, the excellent' (*Mundaka Up.*: II, II, 10-11).

36. 'A *Brahman*a, acknowledging that these worlds are [the outcome] of [accumulated] karma, detaches himself from them, acknowledging that by means of what is perishable one cannot achieve the eternal (*akṛta*: not produced)' (*Ibid.*: I, II,12).

37. Gauḍapāda's *ajātivāda* holds that *māyā* ensures that the reality of dreams and the dreams of reality never evolve towards anything, but disappear completely at the touch of the Realization of the *ātman*.

38. The initiatory Tradition tells us that man is a God... but fallen and involuted; and that from a state of Harmony

he 'fell' to one of disharmony. The task of Realization and of Initiation is precisely that of 'reintegrating' the being to its essential nature.

Therefore man has not 'evolved' but has involuted, and today his involution and degradation are greatly heightened. It is not time that leads the being back to itself, but his awareness and his awakening to what he really is.

39. In a similar way, the Christian Doctrine states that the primordial Adam fell from his harmonious state in paradise and thus weakened his link with God. Christ came on earth to reinstate the 'fallen' man with God.

40. The being can *think* Harmony or disharmony, or what we call good and evil; one is free to make prisons for oneself or to choose liberty; one can direct oneself along unlimited vital possibilities because one is free – by nature – to build one's own destiny.

41. Sooner or later, the human being must become aware of the fact that God does not decide or determine the direction of one's energy.

As long as one fails to recognize oneself as the arbiter of one's destiny, not only does one postpone the solution to the problem of incompleteness, but one creates the alibi of unloading onto a 'personal God' the cause of one's own conflicts and worries.

42. The 'child', who has not yet faced up to its responsibility for its actions, finds it easy to discharge onto others the burden and the consequences of its deeds; but once an adult, one's duty is to become aware of one's own decisions.

43. This world of conflict and suffering is such because man 'believes' it to be so. The more the individuals realize that they are what they think, the more they will be able to 'rectify' the direction of their thinking energies.

44. If man really wants Good and Beauty, all he has to do is to realize them. No individual, capricious God opposes him, and no evil, mischievous demon hinders him.

45. 'Thus the term *awakening* is best suited to this and similar transformations.

Besides, in its modern and especially its idealistic and historical meaning, the notion of 'creating' is influenced by creeping 'evolutionism': it presupposes as a point of departure a kind of 'minus' that has in front of it something capable of increasing it.[1] The initiatory view is the opposite: 'the state of justice' of the being, the original one, ***in signo rationis*** (in the sign of reason), does not have a 'plus', but if anything, a 'minus' on the other side of it (hence the Alexandrian doctrine of the *decrease* in degrees of light in the *próodos*, a term which literally should be translated as 'progress'). Thus there is no talk of becoming god and creator on the part of a non-god and a non-creator ...but instead one speaks of a re-awakening and a re-integration, or of a return to oneself, a 'sleeping God' (Clement of Alexandria), or a 'stunned Angel' (Böhme).

---

[1] We should further underline the fact that the expression 'create a Reality that did not exist before', if taken literally, in the ontological sense and not as an inner experience, would present us with a problem. Because of the before and after, the sentence introduces time in metaphysical reality, while time, at least as we ordinarily conceive of it, is a condition that is limited to the physical state alone.

46. If the empirical or evolution were real, then the Absolute would be determined by the relative and empirical.

If time and space were real, then the timeless Absolute would be conditioned by time.

If the finite and contingent were real, then the Infinite would be limited by the finite.

If the Infinite and the finite, if the Timeless and time, if the Absolute and the relative were both real, there would be two orders of reality within the Principle itself.

If duality were real, we would have a contradiction in the Principle, and this contradiction would annul the Principle.

If duality were real, which one of the two would be the first one?

47. Duality is born of the restless and infant mind of man, who wants to escape from his responsibilities.

48. In the *pariṇāmavāda* (doctrine of 'emanation'), the *ātman* appears to us as the cause of everything; in the *āraṁbhavāda* (evolutionary dualism), the *ātman* appears as *opposed* to our phenomenal reality.

The *vivartavāda* or *ajātivāda* (doctrine of 'non-generation') concludes that empirical reality is neither absolutely real nor unreal, but simple appearance (phenomenon) which, in fact, appears and disappears (*māyā*).

BRAHMAN

49. Of all that is manifest and unmanifest, there is a Principle of absolute simplicity ever-present and all-pervasive. The ṛśis realized it as absolute Silence.

50. *Brahman* is designated as Being, Consciousness, and Bliss. These terms are the expression of man's intellective understanding of it. Pure Being is unqualified (*nirguṇa*), infinite, and fullness. *Brahman* is often indicated as Non-Being as well, because it represents the negation of every attribute, *determination*[1] and classification.

The mind can conceive of some things only in terms of negative or positive; every empirical concept is always a concept of relation, of rapport, but *Brahman* is beyond all relation and all rapport.

51. If the individual were simply the expression of his own empirical mind, he would be unable to embrace *Brahman*.

But he is not just the empirical mind, and so, by opening up to the supra-rational, he manages first to intuit and then to realize *Brahman*.

---

[1] Determination: 4. the determining of bounds; delimitation; definition 1594; in logic, the rendering of a notion more definite by the addition of attributes; also a determining attribute 1644. The Shorter Oxford English Dictionary, vol. I. Clarendon Press, Oxford.

52. Since it represents the Absolute and the One-without-a-second, *Brahman* cannot be *perceived*, thought or conceptualized, but may be simply *realized*.

The essential, ultimate Reality without a second can be *revealed*, but not objectified.

The life of the individual himself can only be realized and revealed, but never objectified. The individual, who is *unity*, cannot split and look upon himself as *other* than himself.

The ultimate unity cannot be split; unity cannot contain in itself opposition, duality, otherness, or contradiction.

There is no other absolute outside of the Absolute.

53. What cannot be understood empirically can be realized through consciousness.

The individual can realize his ultimate Essence because his roots are grounded in it.

If man defines himself as simple relational thought, he can never link himself with his Essence, with the Absolute. 'To think oneself' as mere thought means creating an unbridgeable scission from Reality; it means confining oneself to absolute relativism; in other words, it means considering oneself as 'contradiction'.

54. Those who consider themselves as mere thought and body, believe themselves to be relative and contingent, and living for something relative and contingent is truly paradoxical and senseless.

If a planet or a sun is born, develops and dies, I ask myself: why struggle so desperately when we are faced, not with hope of survival, but with the certainty of death?

What is the sense of worrying about something that tends towards annihilation? One might answer that one fights for the others who are in the same boat with us.

But, my dear brother, those we call 'the others' are as impermanent as you are; and what is the purpose of my services if I see them as cold corpses already?

One may answer that one fights for the generations to come.

But, how can I direct myself at something that does not yet exist? Moreover – even if I did – would not future generations also descend into the abyss of nihilism?

To build a society upon the certainty of its destruction certainly does not spur me to fight.

If a struggle is not an instrument for reaching eternity, it has no bite.

If a struggle does not lead to Life but to death and annihilation, it is a struggle that mocks intelligence and logic.

If the life of human beings did not have a deeper meaning transcending the individualized dimension, it would simply be a hoax and an irrational cruelty. The righteous might well refuse such a life 'without tomorrow'.

55. One must abandon the mind that does not comprehend or that irrationally shuts us in a blind alley, and one must seize the *buddhi* (supra-conscious intuition) which offers unforeseen dimensions and truths that are not of this world.

The sense-based mind lives for the contingent and for illusion; on the one hand, it clings desperately to things and events, and on the other hand forecasts its own death, annihilation, and emptiness.

Those who define themselves as sense-based mind are but living corpses, and because they do not want to regard themselves as such, they seek compensating alibis.

56. *Brahman* is the certainty of your existence, your harbour, the Reality of your own thinking. Your struggle acquires sense because you must *find yourself again*, you

must *awaken*, you must recognize yourself as absolute fullness. *Brahman* is the safe haven for your one-sided, nihilistic mind; it is your immortal Essence and your timeless dimension.

A society makes sense if it tends towards self-discovery, if its action aims at comprehending itself as Bliss, and if its relationships are interwoven with the hope of finding itself once more as vital unity and synthesis.

A society which lives only for its own form, its own body, its needs and its restless desires, is a society without tomorrow, a society that is already dead, although apparently alive, a vegetating society rather than one of wise and knowledgeable beings.

57. *Brahman* is 'not this, not this' (*neti, neti*)[1]; it is not the contingent and mocking pseudo-reality that we have spoken about.

Brahman is '*satyam jñānamanantaṁ*: truth, knowledge and infinity.'[2]

Brahman is beyond all those sophistical arguments of the ignorant, sense-based mind which attempt to demonstrate it or to refute it.

Brahman is exclusively what must be realized, revealed, and experienced, and if we speak of it here, it is in order to stimulate the consciousness to recognize its own immortality.

58. *Brahman* is the *constant*, the absolute, and is not subject to further improvements. *Brahman* is the constant, while the whole of phenomenal life is just a fleeting appearance that can be perceived only because there is the constant. If phenomenon comes and goes, the constant remains. If

---

[1] *Bṛhadāraṇyaka Upaniṣad* II.III.6.
[1] *Taittirīya Upaniṣad* 2.1.3.

your phenomenal bodies come and go, the constant abides in you, and bestows meaning and value on the bodies.

We see the evolution of phenomenal life on our planet because the sun exists as the giver of life and the unchanging constant.

Max Planck, recipient of the Nobel Prize for physics, says: 'Our task is to find in all factors and data the absolute and the universally valid, the invariant concealed in them'.

Well, this is the final aim of *Advaita Vedānta* and of *Asparśayoga*.

'*Neti, neti*' is that operative instrument which spurs you towards the *Brahman*ic constant, the universally valid, the invariant that is behind all vital phenomena, and behind the world of names and forms.

If you fail to see the constant, it is because you are looking only with the sensory eye; you cannot see an electron with the naked eye, but that is no reason to believe it does not exist or that it is unreal.

As in order to see the electron we require appropriate equipment, so in order to 'see' *Brahman* we require a total transformation of the sensory consciousness.

Just as we require appropriate equipment to see the electron, so we require a total transformation of sense-based consciousness in order to 'see' *Brahman*.

59. The solution to your conflict, your suffering, and your contradictions does not lie in promoting moralistic campaigns or changes in social structures; it does not lie in the acquisition of material things and events, but in the realization of *Brahman*, which is your true and profound essence, and in rediscovering your immortality and your inner peace.

Every time you seek to acquire things on the material, emotional or mental plane, this is simply because you are lacking something. Whatever you seek to bring to your 'mouth' as compensation for your lack of completeness is but an evasive pastime which forces you more and more into need and alienation.

A society based on consumerism or on the dictatorship of physical or phenomenal materialism is a society which is avoiding its basic problem and is seeking to benumb itself but not to resolve and rediscover itself. *Brahman* is the constant which solves your conflict, your rapport, your indecision, your thirst for acquisition and your self-assertive violence.

60. There is only one religion: that which leads to the *Brahman* or the Infinite.

There is only one form of politics: that which points to an ethical conduct which is steeped in universalism, in de-emphasising typically material values, and based on the *harmony* of work and capital.

There is only one philosophy: that which is capable of moulding consciousness according to the truth of the *Brahman*ic constant.

There is only one science: that which is able to comprehend the phenomenal illusion of the life of forms, and which sets the universal constant as its ultimate goal.

61. There is only one absolute Reality: *Brahman* **nirguṇa** (the Infinite unqualified or without attributes).

The sense-based human being can conceive of Reality only in terms of humanity, quality, and attribute. Man creates God in his own image: good, bad, loving, powerful, benevolent, chastising, vindictive, tearful, joyful, etc. But these are all attributes inherent in sense-based human nature.

Reality is beyond all qualitative *determinations*, outside of all mental perspectives, however lofty and acceptable they may be.

Reality flees thought which objectifies attributes, tendencies and aims.

62. *Brahman nirguṇa* (Reality or Constant) is the One-without-a-second of the perfectly realized and liberated *advaitin* and *asparśin*. *Brahman saguṇa* (Person) is simply the second for those who have not yet died to all qualification and existential *determination*.[1]

There are those who yearn for authentic union and infinity, and those who yearn for duality and determination.

But between *Brahman nirguṇa* and *saguṇa* there are neither contradictions nor dualisms: these exist only in the mind of the sense-based individual.

Reality cannot be but one, and we all agree on this, I think, but each person conceives of it differently.

Brahman, the Constant can be viewed from many different points of view: as *Saguṇa*, Śiva, Kether, Jehovah, Allah, Kṛśna, Rudra, or Agni; as time and space; as the Unconscious; as the Good, the Beautiful, or the Righteous; as the Infinite; as nothing or the void.

Every son of man adheres to the projection he prefers, and he is capable of fighting and killing to defend his deified projection.

Individualisms, sects, and dictatorships of all kinds come to be and survive thanks to strongly qualified projective actions.

Brahman nirguṇa is behind all these objectifications, the Constant around which rotate all possible time and space projections, the sole and permanent substratum on which all of the manasic lights and shades are painted.

If you love immortality and unity of life, resolve yourself into *Nirguṇa*; if you want to transcend all possible points of

---

[1] See the chapter '*Brahman saguṇa*' in *Tat tvam asi*. Op.cit.

view, resolve yourself into *Nirguṇa*; if you want to resolve the apparent multiplicity of life, sink into *Nirguṇa*; if you want to lay down the weapons of struggle, contradiction, opposition, and distinction, resolve yourself into *Nirguṇa*.

63. You attain *Nirguṇa* through *nirvikalpasamādhi*, and *Saguṇa* through *savikalpa samādhi*.

The former offers the integral, total, universal *solution*; and the latter the experience of union with your objectified Ideal. The second is experience, in the usual sense; and the former cannot be spoken of in terms of dual experience.

Saguṇa neither resolves nor cancels *determinations*, limitations, and distinctions, but harmonizes, unifies and synthesizes them.

Nirguṇa transcends, banishes, and disperses all distinction and characteristic, as the wind disperses mists.

If you have daring and Dignity,[1] cross the abyss and you will re-discover yourself as timeless.

If you are fearful and lack Dignity, you can always integrate yourself in the greatest beauty your soul can conceive.

64. If the Constant is what is permanent, then *phenomenal appearance* is what is inconstant, relative, impermanent and conflictive.

The Constant cannot be annulled by any experience, conceptualization, or event; it is appearance that can be devalued, contradicted and annulled in time and space.

Appearance (*māyā*) can undergo various degrees of evaluation and perspective; let us say, different degrees of truth, which in time and space can be considered real, but

---

[1] For a better understanding of this term, see the chapter 'Sulphureous Dignity' in *The Threefold Pathway of Fire*. Op.cit.

not in the absolute sense; in scientific terms, we might say that it has various systems of co-ordinates.

A cloud in the sky is real, but because it is born and dies, it cannot be considered constant or absolute; therefore it simply corresponds to a certain degree of *relative truth*.

When we look at the moon and, due to a certain trick of the light, we see two moons, we say that our perception is faulty; i.e. we are under an illusion; again, when we see a mirage in the desert we say that it is an optical illusion. This mirage is but another degree of truth ... obviously less true than the former.

When we state that a child has been born of a barren woman, that a dog has horns, or that a circle is square, we are affirming a non-reality; that is, we are in the realm of the untrue.

Just as one system of co-ordinates can be contradicted by another system of co-ordinates, so a relative truth can be contradicted by another relative truth. A cloudy sky is contradicted by a clear, blue one. The dream – relative truth for the dreamer – is contradicted by wakefulness, as light is contradicted by darkness, and the life of forms is contradicted by their death, and so on. Erroneous perception is likewise contradicted by other possible perceptions. We can perceive two moons, or even three. The mirage we perceive in the desert is contradicted by its disappearance.

A relative truth and an apparent truth are, nevertheless, experiential aspects. A dream is a precise experience for the dreaming consciousness, just as observing a mirage is a specific experience. The unreal is what cannot be experienced. An object is unreal when, due to its own self-contradiction, it cannot represent a sensory experiential datum.

The relative or relational truth and the apparent truth constitute *māyā*. To hold that a relative truth or an apparent truth is a self-dependent absolute, that it does not depend on other truths, or that it is self-sufficient, in other words, that *māyā* has its own absolute validity, is to maintain a metaphysical error and fall into ignorance (*avidyā*). Yet many men of 'culture' hold that *half truths* are whole truths.

Every living form cannot avoid being classified as *phenomenon*, that is, as relative truth, and therefore as *māyā*.

Since there cannot be a phenomenon (movement) which depends on itself, absolute Truth is *Brahman* alone.

The universe is 'conformed movement', a formal and vital phenomenon, a mirage, a vast cloud which appears and disappears on the horizon of supreme Truth.

65. Reality, appearance and unreality are the three orders of being and non-being which the human mind can recognize and decide to experience.

These three orders, however, are logical conceptions that allow discernment and distinction: from the point of view of Reality, there is only one Real absolute because all the rest is non-*Brahman*, non-constant.

When all the objectifying of the subject and object is transcended, there is no further datum to be perceived or experienced.

When a dream has been resolved, it ceases to exist; thus, from the point of view of wakefulness, no dream can exist.

When this planet inevitably disappears, vanishing into interstellar space, the clouds will no longer exist, but from the point of view of the absolute Reality there are no clouds.

66. *Māyā* cannot be grasped, because the very moment we observe it, it vanishes. Thus, the moment we consciously seek to perceive and observe a dream, wakefulness takes us to a new kind of experience.

Māyā exists and does not exist. It exists because it is a de facto observation; it does not because it is not constant or real.

67. To say that the universe exists without *Brahman* is like saying that we walk without legs.

We usually affirm, with great certainty, that the universe exists for itself and in itself, that there is no other truth except for what we see as phenomena. In other words, we are declaring that a man can walk without legs or that the light, which gives life to this planet of ours, belongs to the earth and not to the sun.

The greatest conflict human beings have is not the fact that they cannot solve their social problems, but that they live in ignorance (*avidyā*); ignorance concerning the nature of their own essence.

Realization of *Brahman* means the end of all illusion, all relative truths, and all conflicts and sorrows.

68. Those who still identify too much with their passions (whether noble, less noble, or ignoble), their ideals, their relative realities; those who are still disheartened by the hammer of necessity and reactive despair; and those who are still too engrossed in their mental and imaginary philosophical discourses, are not ready for *Brahman*ic Bliss.

Those who are still avidly seeking sensory pleasures and fleeting material riches, who need to give to others what they do not have for themselves, are not ready for *Brahmanic* Completeness.

Every individual, however, in his anguished extroverting turmoil, is in his proper place because, as the *Upaniṣad* states:

'We become what we think.
This is the eternal mystery'.[1]

---

[1] *Maitry Upaniṣad* VI.34.3.

FREEDOM AND SLAVERY

69. The most extreme slavery is the unawareness of being slaves.

The world of slavery is the world of the Self devoid of the Self.

Craving is the source of slavery: Liberty is equanimity in action. If you desire you are not free, and if you desire not to desire, then you still are in slavery.

Alienation, objectification, and outward projection of consciousness mean losing oneself in the mists of *māyā* and *avidyā*, and making oneself the slave of becoming and fragmentation.

Freedom that results from necessity is not true liberty, but only an element of the dialectics of necessity.

70. The disappearance of slavery is disappearance of the objectifying *avidyā*, the solution of the captivating game of conflictive pleasure.

Whoever thinks that from being a slave one should become a *master* has not understood.

Do not seek the chair of command, but try always and solely to be free.

The master is also a slave. Enslaving another means also enslaving oneself.

Master and slave are bound by the same rope: slavery.

The master and the slave form a sad polarity. *Vidyā* (Knowledge) gives you that liberty which transcends all possible polarities.

71. The master is a slave who tries to make slaves of others.

The will for power is merely the will for retaliation of the poor, the servile, the oppressed.

The Liberated man is integrally free; free from human institutions of all orders and levels, free to act or not act; what joins one to other beings is non-binding Love, without passions, gratification or duality.

72. Liberty is liberty not only from masters, conditioned by a thirst for power, but also from those who are slaves, conditioned by mortifying weakness.

73. However much the world may try to enslave him, the Liberated man is always a free being. However much he may be physically constrained, the Liberated man flies free.

74. A*vidyā* often manifests itself as the will for power.

Will for power can be wielded through envy, vanity and even love. A lover can be a passionate oppressor.

75. An individual is the slave of fear, guilt, feelings, his own environment, ideas and fame, his own violence, intelligence, hallucinations and nothingness. The individual is the slave of envy and reaction, his own social position, and his own social and cultural advancement. The individual is born a slave because the nature of the ego is slavery.

True freedom resides beyond this incompleteness, and can be grasped and revealed when the integral consciousness of the being becomes aware of its most profound and unconditioned Essence.

76. That same force that subjugates the slave also subjugates the master. Identification with energy is the source of pain.

The free person makes a servant of nobody, nor has need of flatterers, because he is not devoured by an egoistic will for power, vanity or pride.

A free will is free from everything: even from the idea of freedom itself.

77. One of the most difficult things is to set slaves free, be they masters or servants. Their ego is permeated by *avidyā*, and *avidyā* is a powerful force that bends the back and postpones Asceticism.

Renouncing the Dignity of being and accepting the dissolution into the world of necessity can sometimes relieve one from pain and suffering and may even gratify those instincts and desires that often make one give in and sell oneself.

When the individual has acquired the taste for slavery as a habit, it becomes difficult to smell the perfume of liberty.

78. The way to Liberation may be found beyond all relational concepts of immanence and transcendence, of positive and negative. To fly towards Liberty means not to bow to the dichotomies invented by us, but to Truth, which is the Way, the Door and the Life.

Truth is inseparable from liberty and is sought and revealed through liberty.

Slavery and thirst for power are negations of Truth, and therefore of liberty.

Sooner or later, love for liberty will defeat the deforming and pathological ghost of fear, doubt, and coercive power, and of the past, which is perpetuated in the present.

79. Time enslaves, but Truth defeats time.

Time is memory, past, history, agony attempting to captivate the sympathies of the present. Whoever lives in the past is dead without realizing it.

80. The truly Liberated man lives beyond all the oppositions of subject and object , and beyond all historical and cosmological myth.

The society of the Liberated is a society where Being has rediscovered itself in all its existential integrity.

The society of the Liberated is a society of the Fulfilled. In the society of the Fulfilled there are neither masters nor slaves, because the acquisitive ego that craves and numbs, desires and compares, does not live there.

The task of the Liberated is to prepare the kingdom of liberty, liberty from the ego and the dullness it inexorably engenders.

Slaves cannot prepare the kingdom of fulfilment and liberty. It often happens that their very rebellion simply generates new forms of slavery.

Whoever is a slave of competition, desire, vanity, thirst for power, of conscious or unconscious demagogy, fear, and doubt, cannot prepare the kingdom of Harmony.

It is up to the society of the Liberated to pave the way to order and justice.

81. One must choose between two philosophies: the philosophy which recognizes the primacy of liberty *from* the ego and that which recognizes the primacy of liberty *of* the ego. The former leads to the solution of the prob-

lems of the individual and his relationship with life, while the latter leads to thirst for power, separating pride and violent competitiveness.

Happiness rests on liberty from the ego, on awareness that the individual is a link in the universal chain of being.

The ego of distinction and acquisition cannot generate or determine freedom. As there are lacerations, eruptions, chasms, paradoxes, contradictions, and psychological conflicts, there are no foundations for liberty in the world of the ego.[1]

Liberation means a return to the primordial state, a return to unity. Liberation means reintegrating oneself within the Principle.

82. When the insatiable desire to objectify, gratify and accumulate ceases, then the being discovers its deepest nature, which is joy without object.

In order not to objectify, one must know how to direct one's own energies, understand the dynamics of the psyche, and realize that the individual's goal is not that of gratifying egoistic needs, but of being commensurate with life.

The human being has the task of revealing Harmony, Love and Accord.

---

[1] See the chapter 'Sensory life is conflict' in *Tat tvam asi*. Op. cit.

EDUCATION

83. Rather than teach a culture of history, education in schools should aim at re-educating, by teaching the student to master and reorient the totality of his or her energies (thought, emotions, and instincts).

As long as youngsters are unable to direct their energies harmoniously, they will find themselves in conflict and, as a consequence, will make a conflictive society.

Educational systems in general have a historical approach. Youngsters simply train their memories in the history of philosophy, literature, maths, physics and so on.

A history-oriented education can never produce either creative or integrated individuals.

In Traditional Society education aims at enabling people to comprehend, direct and harmonize their psycho-spiritual energies; it aims at educating consciousness to recognize the fact that individuals must create a bond with life around them because they are an integral part of the life of Being.

84. If the ills of society are called vanity, lust for power, sense of separation, violence, individualistic competitiveness, and so on, then, in order to remove them, one must use a surgical knife and cut them off at the root.

To procrastinate in carrying out this operation means desiring, unconsciously or consciously, an evil that brings suffering in its wake.

Because they aim at the sphere of effects, without touching at all on the deep causes, none of the various policies adopted in order to guide humanity can ever offer a true solution.

Harmony of human relationships depends on the harmony of the individual mind.

Give the individual a harmonious mind and you will obtain a harmonious, integrated society.

85. How can one have a harmonious mind?

First one must be aware of the fact that, depending on its orientation, the mind produces either harmony or disharmony.

On the relative plane neither absolute good nor absolute evil exist; therefore, to contend that the human being is born either good or bad is meaningless. The human being, as such, is capable of producing beauty or ugliness, joy or pain.

To form a harmonious mind, training from a very early age is required. The family should be the first training ground, the school the second, and the individual's working environment the third.

It is obvious that without suitable teachers (in the family, at school, in the work environment, etc.) one cannot conceive of an effective and harmonious programme, as called for by life and reason.

86. Political society on the one hand demands order, harmony and proper relationships, and on the other hand promotes competitiveness, the death of freedom, individualism, and aggressiveness: this represents the contradiction or the paradox of those who lack vision.

Our economic society on the one hand demands that its members implement a policy of 'savings' to finance entrepreneurial endeavours, and on the other hand urges them to indulge in consumerism and acquisition. This is the serpent biting its own tail.

A harmonious relationship between supply and demand leads to economic equilibrium, and a harmonious relationship is the result of the proper education of the individual consciousness.

Controlled and orderly *desires* determine proper political and economic relationships, and so the education of desire must be the prime and immediate aspiration of all peoples.

The highest ethics a man can pursue is that of comprehending, mastering and directing the world of desire as the fire of life and the creator of movement, activity and rapport.

87. The true virtue of a people lies in the proper dosage of desire.

When humanity succeeds in regulating and directing the fire of desire, it will achieve a beneficial osmosis at various levels.

Too much fire can set the social fabric alight; too little fire can make relationships barren and weak.

Those who direct the fire of desire are masters of the fire, and only those who master their own fire can realize well-being and happiness.

88. Those who transcend desire, in all its indefinite expressions, dwell with the Gods.

PROJECTION

89. One must distinguish between *Brahman* in itself and the idea one has of *Brahman*, or between *Brahman* as it is and *Brahman* as an object or a mere mental objectification. Human beings objectify the Real, humanize God and project the idea of good and evil even onto the Absolute.

90. First the individual objectifies God, then makes himself the slave of his own objectification. But the objectified God is outside the individual and his heart, and is an alienated God.

A God created by human limitations is not the Being, but an enslaving phantom that dominates consciousness. The individual is haunted by it and falls a slave to his own restless projection, which is his own *māyā* hallucination.

91. The mind creates the Godhead in its own image and likeness, and attributes to it its own best qualities, but also its worst qualities.

During the entire course of history, we find representations of a God who is both good and evil, both vindictive and loving, human and celestial, spiritual, psychical, and material.

The God who reveals himself to the mind bears the mark of the mind's weakness, the seal of individualism and the lust for power.

92. The objectified God is always a God of strength, assertion, absolutism, and dominion. But the relationship between Person and Being is motivated by union, love and accord. Love does not allow for submission, self-assertion, dominion and abuse; love does not permit weaknesses and incompletenesses of this kind.

Love is harmony of accord and voluntary affinity; it is the union of two subjects and not of a subject and an object. Love shortens distances and annuls differences, it is the merging of essences to the point of identity.

Love is liberty, and it offers liberation because Being is liberty.

Being inspires a sense of liberation and not of submission. Being is love, and love knows no lordship, subjection, difference or supremacy, and not even judgement. Being is not the judge of anyone or the executioner that makes the axe fall on the unjust.

Being is law, harmony, order and beauty, and for those who break the universal laws there are only conflicts.

Liberty is always freedom in conformity with law. Often liberty is mistaken for licence. Sometimes the ego imagines the Being as licentiousness. This again is a projection of what the ego itself would like to do.

Being is harmony, love, and order, and in the nature of harmony there can be no licentiousness of any form or kind whatsoever.

93. Being does not subject anybody; it is the individual that subjects himself with all of his external objectifications and mental representations.

Servile and slavish social relationships are thus transferred to the nature of Being.

To soothe his conscience, the individual transfers to an objectified God all of his own incompleteness and iniquities.

94. Being can be defined by way of symbols, but the mind gives it a voice, qualities and destiny. What triumphs in the alienated theological conception is the exteriorization and objectification of the Essence, and the anthropomorphic, qualitative and quantitative God. Objectification not only distorts the Reality, but also precludes the direct experience of the Divine within oneself.

The image or forms of the Divine, or of ultimate Reality, are hallucinatory events superimposed on *That*. In final analysis they are *māyā*, and in the sphere of *māyā* there cannot be transcendence, love and identity. Objectified transcendence is – paradoxically – what imprisons us within the bonds of the immanent and the coils of necessity.

As long as one idealizes the absolute, one cannot emerge from the relative.

95. The absolute Constant is not an entity or a person, and not even Being, when seen as the origin of a series. In the person, the individual and Being, both micro and macrocosmic, there always is motion and relationship. When the counterpart of the self – as Essence – is projected outwardly, we have the alienated being, which is therefore dual and split and prisoner of its own shadow or ghost.

The Constant or Reality cannot split, or move out of itself, and cannot be given the attributes of change, evolution or thought, and it is not the object of prayer because is not the God of the senses, as would be conceived by the imaginative and individual mind.

96. The individual projects knowledge and harmony outside himself, and then invents the tools or instruments of relationship by which to seek complete fullness. But what can be found and experienced outside oneself will always be some kind of illusory reflection of that true Reality which, instead, is within.

Being, movement, and objectified form and image: one who resolves these three aspects in the transcendent and metaphysical Unity has resolved projection, alienation, conflict and extroverted desire.

One who lives in Unity is beyond the process of becoming, because metaphysical Unity is fullness and completeness, and the Fulfilled man does not seek or desire, and he creates no distinctions.

97. By projecting outwardly, the individual is obliged to build an artificial world in order to compensate for loneliness and alienation.

Gratification of extroverted desire, which is continuously unfulfilled, obliges one, among other things, to become the slave of work and of consumerism at all levels.

One may also be so identified with the artificial and compensatory world that one accepts it as real and absolute. Thus, in order to obtain a moment of pleasure, of self-importance, one desperately clutches at 'shadows' and samsaric phantoms.

The ego lives on miseries and, to avoid its own ruin, forces itself to consider them as the truth.

SOLUTION

98. Once you are freed from name and form, from projecting desire and the conflictive fear they create, what else remains to be done?

99. Sit down, still your mind and meditate deeply on what urges you to think, to project things and events, to build up pride, and seek fame and importance (in the eyes of others), or vanity, and material and erudite or intellectual wealth, etc.
Follow the energy of pleasure or suffering, observe it all as if it were an external object standing in front of you.
Be constant in the practice of observing: for days, months, and years.
While observing, remain a detached observer. Be the point at the centre of your own ebb and flow. You must be like the sun rotating on itself; and you must not allow the force or movement of the energetic contents or planets, which are found in your psychical space, to drag you away.
If you persist, your re-conquered 'solar power' will resolve, to their final dissolution, your lunar powers, which are constricting you.

100. The work proceeds in steps: you must make the solid contents more pliable and, therefore, *liquid* (you

must make the *tamas* become *rajas*). During this phase pay attention to the humidity aspect, for this is of extreme importance. You must *melt* the solid.

Go on now to the next phase: you must make the liquid evaporate and dissolve and thus make it gaseous, that is, *air*. The proper dosage of solar fire and proper *distance* from the content will speed up the operation. During this phase pay great attention: if the Fire is drawn too far away, you will crystallize the liquid without dissolving it; and if you draw closer than necessary, you will bring it to exaltation, and produce scissions, and thus might not be able to withstand the boiling 'emotional sea', and you will burn the whole, with severe consequences.

At this stage of the *Opus*, what you need is vigilance, and an undivided upward direction of energy: release all earthly grips. The proper relationship between solar Fire and strength, or lunar electricity, will complete the whole process.

If you succeed in this operation, you will transform *rajas* into *sattva*, or the emotional, passionate, and repulsing and attracting movement into linear, harmonious and rarefied motion.

If you still have courage, knowledge and a thirst for Unity, then prepare to resolve the air, thought itself. As you can see, I am using the various elements as symbols for deeper realities.

101. This stage is delicate and requires commitment. You have eliminated all objective supports, and now you must eliminate the subjective ones. You have resolved the world of the object, and now you must dissolve that of the subject. Here you are alone with your thoughts and you cannot even *materialize* them because you lack water, the fluid that forges *things*, but also conflicts.

If you harbour aspiration towards *solution*, do not let go, but continue in the opus. Especially at this time, do not look either right or left. Follow the 'Path of the Arrow' and fly towards the solar Unity, the unmanifest or principial Crown.

At this point the action is two-fold: on the one hand, you must burn every idea existing on your planet, by now made just of air. May the Solar Fire dart with its resolving rays. On the other hand, you must begin to live without ... air. Thought itself is of no further use to you. It exists only to solve some individual problems, but, tell me, of what use can such an instrument be to those who no longer have individual problems?

The action of the solar Fire must be incisive and measured; if some reverberation of liquid Fire catches up with you, use vigilance and decision; your aim is to *reduce to ashes* the gaseous seeds that are the roots of ignorance (*avidyā*).

102. Beware: air is subtle, light, darting, but untrustworthy. You think you have it in your grasp, but it is just not so. You believe you have tamed it, and instead you have been subjugated by it; you think you have fooled it, and instead it has fooled you.

Thought is really diabolical; to avoid being burnt to ashes, it is capable of formulating apparently acceptable and flawless philosophical theories for you. Water is too heavy and cumbersome to conceal its movement, but air is shining fire; it knows how to lull you gently, and offers you majestic and inebriating flights.

I tell you that, if you do not dare, you will remain trapped on the plane of air and will have to stay on it for a long time, thus delaying completion of the final work. Many 'thinkers' are delaying it.

But if you are decisive and strong-willed and know how to use the strength of Fire wisely, then you will see the projected rhythm of 'ideals' lessen and slow down.

You can use two very powerful tools: colour and sound. In the final analysis all is light, or more precisely, Fire (Agni), but Fire has many frequencies, many light and sound bandwidths.

With a 'white laser' beam you can *incinerate* a seed to its complete *solution*. Or you can use sound (*mantra*, sentence of power, etc.) and in this case you can crush it and disintegrate it.

Through silence, vigilance and the disintegration of conceptual seeds, you will undoubtedly make progress. If you have completed this process, you have cleared your planetary, air-like substance, and you have made it quiet and still like a deep calm sea.

At this point you are truly with yourself. Oh what sublime reality! But do not believe you are this or that ego, or that same individuality from the past. There is no longer anything in you that once belonged to you. Now you are cosmic living essence, giver of life, and no longer the enjoyer of incompleteness.

You have dissolved all the 'planets' which used to imprison your consciousness, and you remain, therefore, colourless Fire in liberty. You are Agni itself, the god of Fire and of all fires.

103. Now you must put out Fire itself. This passage implies solitude and maturity. It is the final, concluding death; the death that bestows Infinity and Unconditionality. There is no further need to look outside, because nothing stands in front of you any longer. You are alone with yourself and with the *potentiality* of returning again as

air, water, earth or things of another kind, so great is the indefinite expressive possibility you can manifest.

Only at this stage can you realize the true nature and function of *Silence*.

If you become the master of Silence, everything will proceed on its own. Do you comprehend? You have resolved the samsaric, orbital, and translatory movement of your forces, those minor, lunar fires which fed and survived on the heat of the central Fire. Now you must stop even the rotary motion or the central Fire that forces you onto the plane of manifestation, however supra-formal and principial it may be.

If your maturity imposes it on you, then I say to you: *stop* and *wait*.

If you are on the way or in motion and you ask me what to do in order not to move any longer, I will simply answer: stop.

If you ask me what will happen if you stop, I will answer: one who worries about this is not ready yet, and not yet mature. At certain levels one must merely prepare for the agony, without weeping, without speaking, and without asking why. If you have Dignity, then face up to the event; otherwise it is better not to even try.

104. The solid-ferrous element, in the blast furnaces, can be made liquid to such a point that its own molecules will dissociate. Thus we render it gaseous and electronic, and invisible to the sensory eye. If we continue with the work, we can resolve that element into infinite and universal life: mass resolves into free energy.

As you can see, the process is the same. In both cases Fire is the necessary element. In both cases there are certain phases, which have long been known to Alchemy. As below so above, and viceversa.

If you want to play with lead and iron, go ahead: you may obtain material wealth, but you will nonetheless remain incomplete.

If, on the other hand, you consider your own psycho-physical system as the athanor, then things are different: the work requires maturity, dignity and solitude, as well as intelligence and great daring; but if you dare, you no longer require material wealth, because you will win back your absoluteness.

Know that you can follow the Path of Immortality or that of Eternity; the choice is yours.

You can find yourself free to 'descend or ascend' into the various Domains, but you can also transcend all becoming. Remember that also the Gods are steeped in time.

PATH TO AWAKENING

105. Every era has its own call: today's imperative is 'transformation'. What are you waiting for to transform yourself?

The majority classify facts and events. They advance cosmic cycles, and also try to make conjectures about the future. These are historians, chroniclers and, at times, foretellers. They are in time.

If the arrow of *Parca* (Fate) has made you bleed, then draw your solar sword and cut time asunder.

Initiation is not for time-worshippers.

106. You could be wasting your energies, going here and there seeking mystery, and looking for someone in whom to place your vacillating hopes.

Yours is undoubtedly a restless mind and your eyes see uncertainty.

Remember that flight belongs to those who spread their wings in the ether of certainty, decision and univocal surge.

If you think that someone else may remove the thorn from your flesh, know that you are still not ready.

The doctor simply gives prescriptions; the rest is up to the patient.

If worldly emotional restlessness overpowers you, you must clench your jaws and redirect your inner fire.

He who staggers is not worthy of embracing the death of the Philosophers.

107. Are you studying thought processes? Are you acquiring erudition in order to understand that very mind you want to still? Are you wandering about in an attempt to seize dogmas and ideas regarding the mind?
Wake up. He who truly wants to stop, must simply ... stop.
Have you conjured up phantoms which deny you the certainty of Bliss? And now what? Do you let the hammer of your reckless disquiet strike you? Do you still hurt yourself with the spikes of your own mortal thoughts?
Dare. Lift the veil with the Art of accord, and with your Gaze reduce to ashes the enslaving dragon.
In truth I tell you: you were born to grasp the Fire of the supernal World. But if you seek it in faraway regions, then you are mistaken. Turn your investigating gaze inward and allow the all-pervading Fire to consume you.
Transcend your era, debase your mortal destiny, and make the three become one; then follow the phases of the single Fire dying out.
If you have daring, you will know how to get out of the world of necessity, but remember that the Work requires Dignity.

108. If you love the *Qabbālāh*, I shall cry out to you: O you who dwell in Yesod, follow the path of the Arrow, burn in the Fire of *Tiphereth* and dart decisively towards the splendour of Kether, turning neither **right** nor **left**.[1]
Heroes love the snow-covered summits of Ain Soph.

---

[1] For this 'Middle Way' see the chapter 'Metaphysical Path' in Raphael, *The Pathway of Fire according to Qabbālāh*. Aurea Vidyā, New York.

'Ehjeh = I am; *Ahamsi* = I am. Be the Being, and leave the 'attributes' to those who follow the path of the Ancestors.

Kether is the Father, *Tiphereth* the Son and *Yesod* the Holy Spirit.

If you think of operating through the moon of *Yesod* without the sun of *Tiphereth*, then you are on the path of the dead. Some have tried, and others are trying, but their era is marked.

If you possess Dignity and the resolving sword, incarnate yourself as the Son; then fulminate the Father. The 'Pathway of Fire' is the straight road of *suṣumṇā*, not that of *iḍā* or *piṅgalā* or even that of the *svādhiṣṭhāna cakra*.

You approach the nebulous threefold world of *māyā* and you do not realize that the splendour of Bliss awaits you in the *Fourth* or *Turīya* (absolute Essence).

O you who yearn for the Pole, transcend the thinking movement, cut the thread of *avidyā* and sink into the nameless Abyss. To the weak leave the crumbs of support and the deceiving playthings.

109. Love the fearless, exalt the magnanimous, but defend the weak and insecure. The weak are those who fail to master their own restlessness, respond by reacting, use violence, play around with the forces of *avidyā*, waste their own energies, and live on vanity and ambition.

Heroes live and march with composure, measure, and silence in their hearts.

If you fall, do not indulge in tears of commiseration. The Strong may fall, but it is not given to them to wretchedly pity themselves. Dignity is imperative even when falling.

110. Shape yourself in the Fire of Silence, and you will become a strong event-moulding flame. The igneous substance is moulded in the Silence of your strong-willed gait.

If you believe that Will is self-assertion, you are still in *avidyā*.

The world of the Accomplished is not made of weakness and vanity.

If you make silence in your Temple of flesh, sooner or later you will receive direct awareness of the all-pervading Fire which illuminates the symbols of Beauty.

111. Respond to reactive deeds with the magic flashes of meek notes.

A Knight is one who tamed his own horse.

112. If you possess determination, dissolve the precipitous becoming you have promoted; if you dare, you will conquer your immortal polar Centre; if you destroy your tower, you will be the Silence of completeness.

First observe, then dissolve, and then freeze what remains; finally, give way to timeless Bliss. True philosophers tower above history.

The Work is accomplished through the fires of Will and Knowledge. Knowledge which does not reveal Being remains mere imprisoning notion. Will without Knowledge becomes blind brute force.

113. Understanding is one thing, comprehension is another, and realization yet another. The many understand and debate, the few comprehend and meditate, the very few realize and are.

114. Everything is in your hands, and do you still delay? Ask yourself what it is that which you are seeking. Often by realization one means the acquisition of something.

Or are you fantasizing on what you could be in five aeons' time? I dare tell you that you will be today's unfulfilled person if you do not put your hand to the work and do not immediately quench the fire of becoming.

Do not lull yourself into thinking that others will ferry you across to the other side. Trusting 'others' is the childish game of the weak. Know that all what the others can provide you with is a raft.

Observe, dare, deliver the fulminating blow, and stop. After the storm the time of calm always comes.

115. Do you go around begging for vanity, self-assertion and separative pride? My dear mindless one, what game are you playing? Can you not see that the termites are gnawing away at your vital strength and that *avidyā* offers you the crumbs of artificial pleasure? Are you thinking of building a house, a family, and a career? This is simply in order to hide your incompleteness and your solitude.

116. The mind which takes refuge in superstition, in political passion, in a craft, and in the vanity of mundane relationships, sooner or later slides into conflict and pain. A mind which tries to create safe havens for itself on the plane of restlessness is a mind which has not comprehended.

Thinking is process, product, and event; it is time and also space. One who believes in building salvation on discursive and distinctive thought will sooner or later see the entire fabrication collapse.

Thought builds images to play with. It builds images of good, of evil and of political ideals; the image of one's own family, work and silence. But all these images have nothing to do with Reality.

Beauty rejects the contamination of thought.

The creative act is the fruit of illumination and of sudden inspiration, which are not thought. The attention of the traditional Philosopher does not reside in the distinctive mind.

He who aspires to Silence, which is Bliss without object, must transcend thought.

Bliss is revealed only when thought vanishes.

You have the most illusory experience of Silence when thought itself tries to create the image of Silence.

Thought builds images, formulae, projections and dreams, but Reality is not projection, dream or mere image, and is not conceptual representation.

Virtue and every system of ethics built on distinctive ego-centred thought are paths leading to self-gratification.

Ego's virtue is always a hedonistic self-gratification. Often self-dedication is the hedonistic virtue of an ego eager for beggary.

In ego's virtue there is no love, only begging for self-perpetuation.

Love blossoms in the pacified mind.

Hipponion gold-leaf tablet

This is the Work of Memory

When you are about to die, you will go to the well-made halls of Hades.
To the right is a spring, and next to it stands a white cypress.
Coming down to that place, the souls of the dead refresh themselves.
Go nowhere near this spring.
Ahead you will find clear water flowing forth from the Lake of Memory
Over which stand guards, who with keen mind will ask you
What you truly seek in the gloom of deadly Hades.
Say, 'A child of earth and the starry Heaven,
I am parched with thirst and perishing;
But quickly give me cool water flowing from the Lake of Memory.'
They will surely speak to the Queen below the earth
And will give you to drink of the Lake of Memory.
And then may you journey far on the Sacred Way
Travelled by other renowned initiates and devotees of Dionysus.

RAPHAEL

Unity of Tradition

Raphael having attained a synthesis of Knowledge (which is not to be associated with eclecticism or with syncretism) aims at 'presenting' the Universal Tradition in its many Eastern and Western expressions. He has spent a substantial number of years writing and publishing books on the spiritual experience; his works include commentaries on the *Qabbālāh*, Hermeticism, and Alchemy. He has also commented on and compared the Orphic Tradition with the works of Plato, Parmenides, and Plotinus. Furthermore, Raphael is the author of several books on the pathway of non-duality (*Advaita*), which he has translated from the original Sanskrit, offering commentaries on a number of key Vedāntic texts.

With reference to Platonism, Raphael has highlighted the fact that, if we were to draw a parallel between Śaṅkara's *Advaita Vedānta* and a Traditional Western Philosophical Vision, we could refer to the Vision presented by Plato. Drawing such a parallel does not imply a search for reciprocal influences, but rather it points to something of paramount importance: a single Truth, inherent in the doctrines (teachings) of several great thinkers, who, although far apart in time and space, have reached similar and in some cases even identical conclusions.

One notices how Raphael's writings aim to manifest and underscore the Unity of Tradition from the metaphysical perspective. This does not mean that he is in opposition to a dualistic perspective, or to the various religious faiths or 'points of view'.

An embodied real metaphysical Vision cannot be opposed to anything. What counts for Raphael is the unveiling, through living and being, of that level of Truth which one has been able to contemplate.

In the light of the Unity of Tradition Raphael's writings or commentaries offer to the intuition of the reader precise points of correspondence between Eastern and Western Teachings. These points of reference are useful for those who want to address a comparative doctrinal study and to enter the spirit of the Unity of Teaching.

For those who follow either the Eastern or the Western traditional line these correspondences help in comprehending how the *Philosophia Perennis* (Universal Tradition), which has no history and has not been formulated by human minds as such, 'comprehends universal truths that do not belong to any people or any age'. It is only for lack of 'comprehension' or 'synthetic vision' that one particular Branch is considered the only reliable one. From this position there can be only opposition and fanaticism. What degrades the Teaching is sentimental, fanatical devotionalism as well as proud intellectualism, which is critical and sterile, dogmatic and separative.

In Raphael's words: 'For those of us who aim at Realisation, it is our task is to get to the essence of every Teaching, because we know that, just as Truth is one, so Tradition is one even if, just like Truth, Tradition may be viewed from a plurality of apparently different points of view. We must abandon all disquisitions concerning the phenomenal process of becoming, and move onto the plane of Being. In other words, we must have a Philosophy of Being as the foundation of our search and our realisation'.[1]

---

[1] See Raphael, *Tat tvam asi*, (That thou art). Aureā Vidyā, New York

Raphael interprets spiritual practice as a 'Path of Fire'. Here is what he writes: 'The "Path of Fire" is the pathway each disciple follows in all branches of the Tradition; it is the Way of Return. Therefore, it is not the particular teaching of an individual nor a path parallel to the one and only Main Road... After all, every disciple follows his own "Path of Fire", no matter which Branch of the Tradition he belongs to'.

In Raphael's view, what is important is to express through living and being the truth that one has been able to contemplate. Thus, for each being, one's expression of thought and action must be coherent and in agreement with one's own specific *dharma*.

After more than 60 years of teaching, both oral and written, Raphael has withdrawn into *mahāsamādhi*.

* * *

May Raphael's Consciousness, expression of Unity of Tradition, guide and illumine along this Opus all those who donate their *mens informalis* (non-formal mind) to the attainment of the highest known Realization.

PUBLICATIONS

Aurea Vidyā Collection

1. Raphael, *The Threefold Pathway of Fire*, Thoughts that Vibrate for an Alchemical, Æsthetical, and Metaphysical ascesis
Retail ISBN 978-1-931406-00-0
Amazon   978-1-931406-00-0
Apple etal. 978-1-931406-46-8 forthcoming

2. Raphael, *At the Source of Life*, Questions and Answers concerning the Ultimate Reality
Retail ISBN 978-1-931406-01-7
Amazon   979-8-576124-75-6
Apple etal. 978-1-931406-32-1

3. Raphael, *Beyond the illusion of the ego*, Synthesis of a Realizative Process
Retail ISBN 978-1-931406-03-1
Amazon   978-1-931406-03-1
Apple etal. 978-1-931406-18-5 forthcoming

4. Raphael, *Tat tvam asi*, That thou art, The Path of Fire According to the Asparśavāda
Retail ISBN 978-1-931406-02-4
Amazon   979-8-583067-52-7
Apple etal. 978-1-931406-34-5

5. Gauḍapāda, *Māṇḍūkyakārikā*, The Metaphysical Path of *Vedānta**

Retail ISBN 978-1-931406-04-8
Amazon 978-1-931406-04-8
Apple etal. 978-1-931406-45-1 forthcoming

6. Raphael, *Orphism and the Initiatory Tradition*

Retail ISBN 979-8-539590-78-9
Amazon 978-1-931406-05-5
Apple etal. 978-1-931406-35-2

7. Śaṅkara, *Ātmabodha*, Self-knowledge*

Retail ISBN 978-1-931406-06-2
Amazon 978-1-931406-06-2
Apple etal. 978-1-931406-53-6 forthcoming

8. Raphael, *Initiation into the Philosophy of Plato*

Retail ISBN 978-1-931406-07-9
Amazon 978-1-466486-98-0
Apple etal. 978-1-931406-52-9

9. Śaṅkara, *Vivekacūḍāmaṇi*, The Crest-jewel of Discernment*

Retail ISBN 978-1-931406-08-6
Amazon 978-1-931406-08-6
Apple etal. 978-1-931406-48-2 forthcoming

10. *Dṛdṛśyaviveka*, A philosophical investigation into the nature of the 'Seer' and the 'seen'*

Retail ISBN 978-1-931406-09-3
Amazon 979-8-669178-69-7
Apple etal. 978-1-931406-28-4

11. Parmenides, *On the Order of Nature*, Περί φύσεως, For a Philosophical Ascesis*

Retail ISBN 978-1-931406-10-9
Amazon 979-8-698821-95-3
Apple etal. 978-1-931406-22-2

12. Raphael, *The Science of Love*, From the desire of the senses to the Intellect of Love
Retail ISBN 978-1-931406-12-3
Amazon   978-1-931406-12-3
Apple etal. 978-1-931406-54-3 forthcoming

13. Vyāsa, *Bhagavadgītā*, The Celestial Song*
Retail ISBN 978-1-931406-13-0
Amazon   979-8-562809-02-5
Apple etal. 978-1-931406-50-5

14. Raphael, *The Pathway of Fire according to the Qabbālāh* (Ehjeh 'Ašer 'Ehjeh), I am That I am
Retail ISBN 978-1-931406-14-7
Amazon   978-1-931406-14-7
Apple etal. 978-1-931406-49-9 forthcoming

15. Patañjali, *The Regal Way to Realization*, Yogadarśana*
Retail ISBN 978-1-931406-15-4
Amazon   978-1-931406-15-4
Apple etal. 978-1-931406-20-8

16. Raphael, *Beyond Doubt*, Approaches to Non-duality
Retail ISBN 978-1-931406-16-1
Amazon   979-8-657281-16-3
Apple etal. 978-1-931406-25-3

17. Bādarāyaṇa, *Brahmasūtra**
Retail ISBN 978-1-931406-17-8
Amazon   978-1-931406-17-8
Apple etal. 978-1-931406-47-5 forthcoming

18. Śaṅkara, *Aparokṣānubhūti*, Self-realization*
Retail ISBN 978-1-931406-23-9
Amazon   978-1-931406-19-2
Apple etal. 978-1-931406-30-7

19. Raphael, *The Pathway of Non-Duality*, Advaitavāda
Retail ISBN 978-1-931406-21-5
Amazon   979-8-552322-16-9
Apple etal.   978-1-931406-24-6

20. *Five Upaniṣads*, Īśa, Kaivalya, Sarvasāra, Amṛtabindu, Atharvaśira*
Retail ISBN 978-1-931406-26-0
Amazon   978-1-931406-26-0
Apple etal.   978-1-931406-29-1

21. Raphael, *The Philosophy of Being,* A conception of life for coming out of the turmoil of individual and social conflict
Retail ISBN 978-1-931406-27-7
Amazon   979-8-630006-39-4
Apple etal.   978-1-931406-31-4

22. Raphael, *Awakening*
Retail ISBN 978-1-931406-44-4
Amazon   979-8-716953-07-9
Apple etal.   978-1-931406-33-8

Related Publications

Śaṅkara, A brief biography
Aurea Vidyā. New York.
Retail ISBN 978-1-931406-11-6
Amazon   978-1-931406-11-6

Forthcoming Publications

Śaṅkara, *Brief Works*, Treatises and Hymns*

Retail ISBN 978-1-931406-71-0
Amazon 978-1-931406-55-0
Apple etal. 978-1-931406-56-7

Māṇḍūkya Upaniṣad, with the Gauḍapāda's *kārikā*s and the Commentary of Śaṅkara*

Retail ISBN 978-1-931406-37-6
Amazon 978-1-931406-57-4
Apple etal. 978-1-931406-58-1

*Upaniṣads**

Retail ISBN 978-1-931406-38-3
Amazon 978-1-931406-59-8
Apple etal. 978-1-931406-60-4

Raphael, *Essence and Purpose of Yoga*, The Initiatory Pathways to the Transcendent

Retail ISBN 978-1-931406-36-9
Amazon 978-1-931406-61-1
Apple etal. 978-1-931406-62-8

Self-knowledge, The Harmonization of Psychic Energy. Edited by the Kevala Group

Retail ISBN 978-1-931406-40-6
Amazon 978-1-931406-63-5
Apple etal. 978-1-931406-64-2

*Uttaragītā**

Retail ISBN 978-1-931406-68-0
Amazon 978-1-931406-69-7
Apple etal. 978-1-931406-70-3

Sanskrit Glossary
Retail ISBN 978-1-931406-67-3
Amazon   978-1-931406-65-9
Apple etal. 978-1-931406-66-6

* Translation from Sanskrit or Greek and Commentary by Raphael.

Aurea Vidyā is the Publishing House of the Parmenides Traditional Philosophy Foundation, a Not-for-Profit Organization whose purpose is to make Perennial Philosophy accessible.

The Foundation goes about its purpose in a number of ways: by publishing and distributing Traditional Philosophy texts with Aurea Vidyā, by offering individual and group encounters, by providing a Reading Room and daily Meditations, at its Center.

* * *

Those readers who have an interest in Traditional Philosophy are welcome to contact the Foundation at: parmenides.foundation@earthlink.net.

Printed in Great Britain
by Amazon